Melvin Van Peebles'

WATER-MELON MAN

by

Andrew J. Rausch

Foreword by

Rob St. Mary

Melvin Van Peebles' Watermelon Man
By Andrew J. Rausch

Published in the USA by:
BearManor Media
1317 Edgewater Dr #110
Orlando, FL 32804
www.bearmanormedia.com

Perfect ISBN: 979-8-88771-167-6
Case ISBN: 979-8-88771-168-3
BearManor Media, Orlando, Florida
Printed in the United States of America
Book design by Robbie Adkins, www.adkinsconsult.com
Front cover photo appears courtesy of Photofest, 2023
Back cover photo courtesy of Dreamstime, 2023

This book is dedicated to the complicated, complex, and incomparable Melvin Van Peebles. Love him or hate him, he was one of a kind.

ALTHEA GERBER: Aren't you concerned with the civil rights issue?

JEFF GERBER: Yeah, sure. Most people are just crazy! They think that at any moment a negro's just going to hit them over the head with a watermelon and steal their high school ring.

(Dialogue from *Watermelon Man*)

JEFF GERBER: What happened to the flaming liberal I was married to?

ALTHEA GERBER: I'm still liberal, but to a point.

(More dialogue from *Watermelon Man*)

TABLE OF CONTENTS

Foreword: Then Again, Maybe You *Should* Show This Film to a Third Grader

by Rob St. Mary

Growing up working class in Metro Detroit, you come to understand race is an aspect of life even before you can articulate it. That was especially true as someone born in the late 1970s, about a decade after hundreds of thousands of white people fled the city for the suburbs following the 1967 rebellion. Those days in July in the Motor City became the biggest rebellion since the draft riots during the Civil War in New York City over one hundred years before and was only eclipsed by the L.A. uprising in 1992. During my elementary school days, there was only one black student in our school. One of my earliest memories of racial talk in my neighborhood was a first grade friend who lived a block over who told me his family didn't watch *The Cosby Show* (in the mid-1980s before we knew what a predator Bill allegedly was) because "there are n*****s on that show." He said that vile slur as casually as one might give the time of day. My family didn't abide such talk. My father always chafed against racism and made the point to me at a young age that "there are assholes of all colors and backgrounds—never forget that." I guess that was his way of asking me to remember Dr. King's hope that his children one day will "not be judged by the color of their skin but by the content of their character."

I don't know how much my parents paid or the exact date we got our VCR, but it must have been around five hundred dollars in 1987 or 1988 dollars (or about $1,200 in 2021, according to an online inflation calculator). But I'll never forget the first two films I saw in my home on VHS was because of my dad's insistence that we needed to watch them as soon as possible because they were movies he had seen during his basic training in the US Army while stationed at Fort Benning, Georgia in 1971. Little did

I know these two movies would profoundly impact me throughout my life as a human, writer, and all-around film geek. They were Stanley Kubrick's *A Clockwork Orange* and Melvin Van Peebles's *Watermelon Man*.

Depending on when this double feature happened, I was nine or ten years old. At the time, it probably wasn't the best choice my father made to show me these films at such a young age. But then again, maybe he realized there was something in them that I needed to know even though he had only seen them once, well over a decade earlier. Perhaps he knew that as I was on the cusp of moving out of childhood and into understanding the cruelty that comes with the teen years and adulthood, and that these stories offered something the latest Disney film didn't. Thinking about it now, Kubrick's film offers a lens on questions of delinquency, crime, punishment, and the concept of individual will, and if we could take away the choice for evil, we would also take away the choice for good at the same time. Van Peebles' film offers something else—a way for someone like me, growing up where I did, to understand bigotry, racism, and the hate that hate can produce.

At its core, *Watermelon Man* is a version of Franz Kafka's *Metamorphosis*, but instead of a man waking up as an insect, he wakes up black. Jeff Gerber is the average, casual white bigot. What I mean by casual bigot is he's not the type of person to burn a cross on someone's lawn or commit a direct act of terrorism against black people, but he sure as hell thinks that group of people is always "playing the race card" and should "know their place." Sadly, I grew up around many men like him in my old neighborhood who think nothing of making comments about people of color, gays, women, or anyone else who is not them, and when you call them on it, these bigots hide behind it being a joke and you're just too sensitive.

The way Melvin builds the story is classical in many ways. We meet Jeff, the family, the daily routine, and then something happens that throws it all into chaos for someone who was perfectly content living the American dream in his white suburban neighborhood. Slowly, almost so you don't notice it, you start to genuinely feel for

Jeff in a masterful performance by comedian Godfrey Cambridge both in and out of whiteface.

To put it bluntly, Jeff has been an asshole, and even though he becomes black, he's still boorish and pushy, carrying around a heavy load of "white privilege" that seeps from his every pore. After being thought of as a thief for trying to continue his daily exercise routine while black, he is later shunned by his neighbors telling him to move out. Even his own wife can't handle Jeff this way. In many ways, Estelle Parsons's "Althea" is a stand-in for the good liberal—then and today. If you think the people on the Right roast such people in the age of woke, Melvin understands how someone like Althea means well but doesn't stand strong during a real crisis in the cause of equality for black people. The reason why she can't bring herself to commit fully is that she's too concerned about what the neighbors or her family will think rather than the importance of human rights and dignity. She can't stand Jeff's tone, and how he fights for his equality by using the neighbors' racism to milk every dollar he can get out of them when they want to buy his house to get him out of their lily-white neighborhood. Before, Althea just grinned and bore Jeff's boorishness. But that was when he was a white asshole. Melvin shows us how society will accept such a crude and horrible person but not someone living their life, or trying to at least, as an average black man in American society.

Althea and the kids leaving Jeff didn't make me sad; in fact, I think that might have been for the best. But things start to get heartbreaking when his doctor tells Jeff he doesn't want him as a patient anymore. Then, he faces being fetishized for the first time at the hands of Erika, the sexy Swede from the office. Melvin shows us that getting attention because of a fluke of DNA instead of who you are as a person is just as shattering as being hated for the same reason. As Jeff's understanding, or to use a more political phrase—consciousness, is raised, he finds himself closer and closer to what was then called the "Black Power" movement, typified during the film's era by the Black Panther Party for Self-Defence—a direct reaction to police brutally which started in Oakland, California and then fanned out throughout the country. In the last shot, a freeze-frame recalling Truffaut's *The 400 Blows*,

Melvin indicts society in a shot that says, "Look what you did. I am the hate that hate produced."

Did I realize the depth of *Watermelon Man* when I saw it over thirty years ago?

No, and I don't think my dad did either. But in recent years, I've come to appreciate just how structured this film is without really hitting you over the head. I think if this were in the hands of a lesser filmmaker, it would have come off as stiff or even offensive, especially with the original ending—I'm sure someone will talk about that later in this book. But in Melvin's hands, as a storyteller, it plays smoothly and creates a surrealistic, funhouse mirror-type world in which many of the great satires play while being relatable and lived-in.

It might sound odd, but as I have gotten older, I realize I relate to Jeff, the black version. Thinking back on when I saw it the first time as a child, I understood what it was like to be excluded and put upon by the expectations of others. I was often bullied in the schoolyard, and it was because I was either the fattest and/or tallest kid in my class. This led to a lot of fights, whether I wanted them or not. This pugilistic childhood ran from Kindergarten until about seventh grade. So, I always felt this social hate for something that didn't really seem like my fault. I wasn't particularly loud like Jeff, but I still used humor as a defense. So, another reason why this film resonates so much for me is that I can relate to this feeling that I was someone who was a threat but never understood why. That's probably another reason I related to James Whale's *Frankenstein* starring Boris Karloff. Anyhow, by the time Jeff gets to the point that he does understand how this society works, it makes sense that he would join a group like the Black Panthers. When you have been hurt so deeply for no real reason besides fear, it feels like there could be no other ending that would satisfy and make the point, as I noted earlier, the hate that hate produced.

This is not to say I know anything about the black experience in America. I am a very white man with my mother coming from one of the whitest countries on the planet—Scotland. The people who trace their lineage back to the clans of the isles know their skin tone is as pale as the Klansman's robes that, sadly, many who share my heritage donned over America's history. But by talking to close friends and their families over my life, as well as reading, I can say I understand the challenges of black and other marginalized people in American society. That's why I've always felt much closer to people who have been raised in a similar "factory rat" working-class background who survive paycheck-to-paycheck than I have ever felt with people who share the same skin tone as me. That might be why this movie still resonates, and we need its lessons now more than ever. Not only the black/white issues but the queer/straight issues and all the divisions in between. Because if we can give ourselves and each other some empathy, especially when we meet someone as originally unlikable as Jeff Gerber, we might just see ourselves and how we can help redirect and reconnect them to the universals of humanity.

I love this film, but it makes me sad to think you could pretty much remake this film today with just a few dialogue tweaks, modern dress, and it would still play to a lot of the same issues. Fifty years is a long time, and we've come a long way, but there's still a long way to go. *Watermelon Man* feels contemporary, and you could even make the case that it is a spiritual father to something like Boots Riley's extraordinary *Sorry to Bother You*—a film that picks up where Melvin leaves off about what it means to live as a black person in America.

So, for all the inappropriate aspects of showing *A Clockwork Orange* and *Watermelon Man* to a pre-teen in the late 1980s, I have to say, "thanks, dad!" While I believe both films were a shock to my system, I see them as the start of my moral education. As a Humanist, I believe we must figure out how to make this world work for all, or we will suffer even more than we already are. We need to see our responsibility to understand and embrace each other, or else we will always be running this absurd race that never really gets us anywhere, kind of like Jeff racing the bus—a meaningless symbolic victory that does nothing but breed contempt.

Introduction: WHY WATERMELON MAN?

by Andrew J. Rausch

"Why *Watermelon Man*?" This is a question I was asked repeatedly while writing and assembling this volume. The question is fair enough, I suppose. After all, *Watermelon Man* is hardly *Citizen Kane* (or any other perceived masterpiece). No one, including the film's writer, director, producer, or stars, has been so bold as to identify it as such. I'm sure someone out there believes *Watermelon Man* is a masterwork, but labeling it as such requires a good deal of mental gymnastics and a reconsideration of the criterion by which films are judged. So, you might posit the question once more: "Why *Watermelon Man*?" To this, I would answer, why <u>not</u> *Watermelon Man*? One might be inclined to call this a piss-poor response and a cop-out, and I would be the last to argue.

Okay, so we've established that the film isn't a masterpiece, but who gives a damn? *Watermelon Man* possesses a fair amount of artistic merit (even if it is a tad rough around the edges), and it holds a place in history as one of the first studio films made by a black filmmaker. (Some sources identify it as the first, but that is incorrect.) Moreover, *Watermelon Man* is a fun film. It was also the first studio film on which minorities were hired to shadow and learn at all the significant crew positions; this decision, allegedly by Van Peebles himself, had an immediate effect as it resulted in a handful of new minority film talent (where there had previously been next to none).

Beyond that, *Watermelon Man* is a key (and telling) event in the life and career of Melvin Van Peebles. The director is widely praised for kicking off the black film cycle of the 1970s (or "the black film revolution," if you will) with *Sweet Sweetback's Baadasssss Song*. As such, the director's sole completed studio effort and predecessor to *Sweetback* often gets lost in a discussion of the man's contributions to cinema. One of the biggest successes of *Watermelon Man* was its becoming a springboard for Van Peebles as a known American filmmaker, as well as a project around which he was able to establish (and I suspect construct through a bit of historical rewriting) his larger-than-life persona as a "take no shit" non-compromising black auteur. Much of his legendary reputation as such is the product of tales he frequently spun about how Columbia had attempted to sucker him and how he wound up suckering *them*.

When scrutinized, some of the tales Van Peebles liked to tell about the film's creation seem contrived. Nevertheless, the stories are good ones, and they help to reaffirm his image as the Godfather of Black Cinema. Let's take a look at some of these likely tall tales. For starters, Van Peebles' claim that (1) he was concerned that the studios would view him as being a representative of all black filmmakers and, as such, wanted him to fail so they wouldn't have to hire any more minority directors does not jibe with his claims about how he then fooled the studio by misrepresenting his plans and actions regarding the film's ending, forcing them to use an ending they didn't like. If Van Peebles genuinely believed that the future of black filmmaking at the studios rested on his shoulders and was dependent on his actions (which it may well have been), then his alleged trickery makes no sense. Other Van Peebles tales seem equally implausible. For instance, he often told a story about his hiring a black shoe shine man at Columbia Pictures because he *knew* the studio execs would ask the man his opinion on *Watermelon Man*.

Furthermore, according to Van Peebles, they did. This story is problematic for several reasons, not the least of which is Van Peebles' astounding foresight that the studio would ask this man for his opinion. (This seems particularly far-fetched considering that there was no precedent for Van Peebles to look to in making this assumption.) Also, how exactly would Van Peebles go about replacing the studio's existing shoe shine man with a hand-picked man of his own? The logistics of this are questionable at best. Nevertheless, it makes for one hell of a story, and Van Peebles was nothing if not a good storyteller.

The filmmaker's legend also benefitted from the public perception that he refused to return to work for the studios. (He later worked on the Richard Pryor vehicle *Greased Lightning* but was replaced by Michael Shultz with the studio citing "artistic differences.") I am not sure that Van Peebles ever flat-out stated he had refused to work for the studios after *Watermelon Man*, but he did little to dispel the notion. And why should he? This misperception helped him to achieve notoriety and helped solidify his image as a black artist who stood up to The Man and knocked down every barrier that stood in his way.

Pointing these things out is not meant to diminish Van Peebles' importance. These observations are only chunks of the road upon which I travel to reach my point. Van Peebles is a legend and is undeniably an important figure in cinematic history. Whether or not he was the defiant renegade he has painted himself to be (at least to the degree he claims) is irrelevant. In this instance, the *image* is king. Because the image that Van Peebles portrayed (whether earned, cultivated, or some combination of both) served as an inspiration for future black filmmakers. As I stated previously regarding my observations being "chunks in the road" to reach my point, Van Peebles' image, reputation, and career was the road upon which a community of black artists traveled to become professional filmmakers. Consider how Van Peebles' image as a strong black filmmaker must have appeared to young black people at the time (as well as the generations who have since followed). If those young people had aspired to make films, Van Peebles served as a concrete example that the dream was attainable. Even if these young people had never considered filmmaking prior to this (likely because they would have dismissed such a notion as an impossibility), Van Peebles was living proof that they could do anything they wanted to do.

Moreover, the example Van Peebles provided reaches far beyond filmmaking. He was a Renaissance Man with a ridiculous number of astonishing accomplishments under his belt; accomplishments that would have seemed impossible for *any* man, let alone a black man living in 1960s and early 70s America. No matter what anyone may think about Van Peebles or his art, there can be no denying that he found a way to do just about everything he set his sights on doing. After graduating with a B.A. in Literature from Ohio

Wesleyan University, he served a stint in the Air Force. After that, he lived in Belgium, where he studied astronomy. Having already published a photo/essay book titled *The Big Heart* at the age of twenty-five, he relocated to Paris, where he taught himself to read and write French and then published five books in the language. During this time, Van Peebles also wrote several plays and became prominent enough that author Chester Himes helped him secure a job as a columnist (and later editor) for the anti-authoritarian publication *Hara-kiri*.

Not a man to rest on his laurels, Van Peebles began making music and released his first album, *Brer Soul*, on which he performed a sort of spoken word/singing hybrid. (Many hip-hop artists would later speak of his influence on their music and the art form itself.) Van Peebles next figured out a way to make a motion picture, so he adapted his novel, *La Permission*, as *The Story of a Three-Day Pass*. This landed him his first professional filmmaking gig with *Watermelon Man*. After that, he wrote and directed *Sweet Sweetback's Baadasssss Song*, which became a hit and forever changed black filmmaking. The rough aesthetics of the film are often discussed, but not nearly enough attention is given to the fact that Van Peebles taught himself to make films. In fact, he taught himself to do all the fantastical things he did in his lifetime. The man even taught himself about the stock exchange and went to work for a time as the first black options trader on the floor of the American Stock Exchange. He is frequently cited as being a revolutionary figure. However, hardly any attention is given to the revolutionary nature of Van Peebles *teaching himself to do things* and then *doing them* without waiting for opportunities to be offered. Melvin Van Peebles *created his own* opportunities, setting an example from which we could all learn.

The story of *Watermelon Man* is a story of Melvin Van Peebles. It is but a single chapter in the man's extraordinary life and career. This book is intended as a celebration of both the outrageous 1970 film and the even more outrageous 1932-2021 Melvin Van Peebles. As of this writing, a proper print biography of his life does not exist. So, until such a volume emerges, this book will have to suffice.

AUTHOR'S NOTE

This book was challenging to construct because most of the individuals who worked on *Watermelon Man* are now dead and gone. I made numerous attempts to interview Melvin Van Peebles and screenwriter Herman Raucher. I was told by a mutual friend that Van Peebles was sick, so it was not a surprise when he did not respond. Raucher declined multiple times (through a representative). (It probably didn't help matters that he reportedly hates the finished film.) Van Peebles passed away shortly after my request. Despite this, an interview I had conducted with him previously is included here.

I must warn you upfront that there are quite a few repetitive statements made by different people in different contexts within these pages. This is partially because of the number one hurdle I faced with this book, which was that there wasn't a lot of detailed information out there about the making of the film. Most of the film's primaries made the same one or two passing remarks about the project, and Van Peebles pretty much stuck to reciting the same couple of well-worn stories.

Another interesting aspect of this project is that the interviews, quotations, and lore often contradict one another. Because there was no real way to verify the statements, I decided to include them all. Much like an oral history (and I have written a couple of those), the contradictions leave it up to the reader to determine what they believe to be true.

I want to thank the following individuals for their assistance with this project: Ben Ohmart, Rob St. Mary, Mike White, Joshua Weathersby, Cassius Weathersby, John B. Bennett, Michael A. Gonzales, Ivan C. Beckoff, Garrett Chaffin-Quiray, Novotny Lawrence, Donna Dubrow, Nat Segaloff, Michael H. Price, and Michael Ferris.

AN INTERVIEW WITH MELVIN VAN PEEBLES

You can't have a serious discussion about the blaxploitation cycle without mentioning Melvin Van Peebles. It would be like talking about the Bible and not mentioning Jesus. Van Peebles, who has been dubbed the Godfather of Black Cinema, made his earliest short films in 1957. Van Peebles then traveled to France, where he found success as a novelist. In 1968, he directed his first feature-length film, *The Story of a Three-Day Pass*. The film, which Van Peebles made in French, garnered him accolades and awards. He then followed this achievement with his first Hollywood production, the 1970 comedy *Watermelon Man*. The film, written by Herman Raucher, told the story of a casually racist white man who wakes up one morning to find that he has somehow been transformed into a black man.

However, it would be Van Peebles' next film, *Sweet Sweetback's Baadassss Song*, for which he would be most remembered. The now legendary independent film was written, directed, produced, composed by and starred Van Peebles. The film, which Van Peebles dedicated to "all the Brothers and Sisters who had enough of the Man," was a major indie success and is generally considered the first blaxploitation film.

Van Peebles has since helmed a number of films, including *Don't Play Us Cheap* and *Gang in Blue*, which he co-directed with his son Mario Van Peebles. In addition, he has found significant success as both an actor and a musician. Van Peebles is also the author of the book *Sweet Sweetback's Baadassss Song: A Guerrilla Filmmaking Manifesto*, and is the subject of the films *Baadasssss!* (2003) and *How to Eat Your Watermelon in White Company and Enjoy It* (2005).

It should be noted that, because this interview was conducted for my 2011 book Reflections on Blaxploitation *(co-written and edited with David Walker and Chris Watson), its scope reaches beyond* Watermelon

Man *(although a portion of it does appear inside the booklet for the Indicator Blu-Ray release of the film and was later quoted in the liner notes of the 2022 re-release of the film's soundtrack.)*

ANDREW J. RAUSCH: *Tell me about your path to becoming a filmmaker.*

MELVIN VAN PEEBLES: I wrote a photo essay about my having worked as a grip man on a cable car in San Francisco. I'd wanted to be a writer, and I thought I had a unique perspective regarding this particular story. So one day, a guy goes on my cable car and he's asking me questions about the essay. My real name is Melvin Van Peebles, but I think he expected it to be something like Leroy Johnson. [Laughs.] So he didn't think I had written the essay. And so he said, "Well, who set up these angles in these photographs?" And I said, "I did." And he said, "Well, who wrote the text?" I said, "I did." "Well, who did the layout?" I said, "What's layout?" He said, "That's how you lay the page out." And I said, "I did." And he was dumbfounded. He said, "It just reads right along. It's like a movie." And I thought, shit, I should make a movie. And that's how I became a filmmaker.

I found a guy who had a camera, and he said I could use it if I took him and made him the director of photography, whatever the fuck that was. So I said, "Sure, okay." And I made my first film, and I projected it up on the wall. He said, "We haven't edited yet." I said, "What's that mean?" So someone gave me Eisenstein's *Film and Form*, and that book consisted of my film education. Period. That was all I ever had.

My first "feature" turned out to only be eleven minutes long, but what the hell? [Laughs again.]

AR: *You made your first full-length film,* The Story of a Three-Day Pass, *in France. How did that come about?*

MVP: Well, back before they had videocassettes and DVD's, they used to have film nights in gyms and auditoriums for film fanatics in the States. And there was this guy named Amos Vogel, who's still around, and he used to take films out and show them around the country. He was a film fanatic before it became *de rigeur* to be such. And the Cinemateque in France invited him to come and screen some of his films there. And I had leased my first few short films with him while I was on my way to Europe, where I was getting my Ph.D in astronomy. So Amos Vogel took these films there and screened them, and the French loved them. They then looked me up and sent me a letter in Holland. They said, "Wow, why aren't you making more films?" Well, I had gone down to Hollywood, but Hollywood was very lily white at the time. There was no chance of getting in. So I had gone back to my first love, which was celestial mechanics, which is a type of mathematics and astronomy.

So anyway, I go to France, and they were very nice to me. They screened my films, everybody kissed me, and then they drove off. And I'm standing there with two wet cheeks, three cans of film, not able to speak a single word of French, and not having a penny in my pocket. So I decided right then that I was either going to make it or die there in France. So, little by little, I learned French through immersion. Then I discovered that there was a French law that said a French writer could have a temporary's director's card. So I wrote and published five novels in French and then asked for my director's card.

And there you are.

AR: *Could you tell me about the genesis of* Watermelon Man*?*

MVP: I was at Universal. My film *The Story of a Three-Day Pass* had won the Critic's Choice Award at the San Francisco Film Festival. I had returned to San Francisco as a French delegate. Nobody had known that I was American, let alone a black American. So from there, I was knocking around Hollywood, which was suddenly opening its doors to me. And my agent called me and said he had a script for me titled *The Night the Sun Came Out on Sleepy Hollow Lane*. He named several actors who were interested: Jack Lemmon, Alan Arkin. But none of the actors had seemed right yet. So he sent me the script so I could read it over the weekend. I called him on Monday and said, "I think you sent me the wrong script." And he asked why. "This character's black." And he said, "Yeah, but he's white for the first five minutes." And I said, "Well, why don't you get a black guy to play a white character in whiteface instead of a white guy to play a black character in blackface? Is that possible? And that's how that project came about.

AR: *I understand the original ending of* Watermelon Man *was quite a bit different in the screenplay. Could you tell me about that?*

MVP: Well, he goes to take another shit and he wakes up and he's white again. It was all a bad dream.

AR: *You've scored all of your films yourself. Did you have any formal training prior to that, or did you just kind of teach yourself the way you did filmmaking?*

MVP: I still don't have any training. If it ain't broke, don't fix it! I numbered all the keys on the piano, all eighty-six, because the piano was missing two keys. And I just started pecking away the melody I heard inside my head. And even today, I go into the studio and the guy says, "Oh, you wrote that in D minor? Blah, blah, blah." And I just say, "What the fuck do I know about any of that? Just play it."

AR: *Let's talk about* Sweet Sweetback's Baadasssss Song, *which you made yourself. What was the budget on that picture and how did you raise the money?*

MVP: I've never told anyone the budget. And the money was mine. I own everything, and I have no partners on that.

AR: *I read that Bill Cosby played some role in financing?*

MVP: Yes. He loaned me some money. Toward the end there, I needed some money. Bill stepped in and loaned me fifty grand, which I repaid to him rather than giving him a piece of the film.

AR: *Tell me about the distribution of* Sweet Sweetback's Baadassss Song.

MVP: Everybody turned it down, so forth and so on. Then a company called Cinemation came along. They were in Chapter eleven and they took it. Only two theaters in the entire United States would show it. Not even two cities, but two *theaters*! [Laughs.] And it broke box-office records at both theaters immediately. After that, of course, everybody called me. And the company was not set up to hide the money, so I got the money. They couldn't afford any carpets to hide the money under at the time.

AR: *Different people call you a lot of different things: a rebel, a pioneer. Spike Lee has dubbed you the Godfather of Black Cinema. How do you see yourself?*

MVP: I'm not really much of a navel-looker. I have this method I live by. I have the newspaper delivered to me in the morning. I look in the obituary column each morning. If I'm not in there, then I get my ass up.

AR: *You made a documentary about the history of black cinema,* Classified X. *How did that come about?*

MVP: A French company asked me if I wanted to make an anthology film about blacks in Hollywood. I said, "No. I'm not interested in that. But I will tell you the story I want to tell. You want that, fine, I'll make that. But I will make it my way and I make the decisions. I'm the boss or I'm not making it."

So I made sure I was the boss. I'm also the producer and the narrator, and I also own fifty percent of the print. So I got to be the boss and do it the way I wanted to do it. People say, "Why don't you try to get American money?" I say, "Bullshit. I don't want American money. I'd rather be the boss and make what I want to make, the way I want to make it."

AR: *Your son, Mario Van Peebles, directed the feature film* Badassss! *about you. You've also been the focus of numerous books and documentaries. That must be quite surreal.*

MVP: When I first saw my son Mario's film, I said, "It's Seabiscuit on two legs." [Laughs.] I've become Seabiscuit!

AR: *You've become quite a cult figure.*

MVP: You know, I don't think it could happen to a nicer guy! [Laughs again.] People say, "You're so brave" or "you're so tough." I'm not. I'm not anything. It was like that movie *Network*; I just wasn't going to take it anymore. People say, "How are you doing this?" or "It must be so difficult." Nope. It's not difficult at all. I just do it.

THE FILMMAKERS REFLECT ON *WATERMELON MAN*

MELVIN VAN PEEBLES: [The studios] were still pursuing me, so I said, 'Okay, I'll come,' because it was time for the next step. I said, 'I'll shoot *Watermelon Man* if we shoot it in Hollywood,' which they agreed to do. I felt it was the next political barrier to break down.

So I made *Watermelon Man*; there are a gazillion hilarious stories about that. This guy called me up and gave me the script. We've talked to some people, he mentioned Jack Lemmon, Alan Arkin, and they were trying to find just the right guy. I read the script. I called him and said, 'I think you sent me the wrong script.' He said, 'What is it?'''The guy's black.' 'Yes, but he starts off white.' 'So get a black guy to play it in white face.' 'Is that possible?' They were perfectly willing to get a white guy to play in black face but could a black guy play a white man? They put me through all kinds of hell. Tests, this and that, makeup test. They gave me a lot of latitude out of . . . it didn't dawn on them that I might be cleverer than they were.

For example, in the original script, *Watermelon Man* ends with the guy having to get up in the middle of the night and then he's white again, it was all a bad dream. I said, 'I don't find that ending acceptable.' We're sitting around a room with a bunch of executives. What are you going to do? 'We'll shoot it both ways. Okay, Mel, we'll do that and we'll see later on.' They gave me twenty-three days to shoot *Watermelon Man*. They programmed me for failure. As soon as I realized they were trying to fuck me, I shot it in twenty-one days and I shot things all out of sequence, so they couldn't follow what I was doing, so they couldn't start fucking with me. I'll never forget it. About day twenty, the guys came down, 'Mel, just came down to see how things are going. How many extra days are you going to need?' I said, 'Didn't you get my card for the wrap party? Day after tomorrow.' Then, during editing, the guy calls me, 'Mel, the other ending, we want to try that out and see how it works.'

The other ending? 'Yeah, you know where he wakes up . . .' 'Lawd have mercy, this colored boy done forgot to shoot that part. Oh, lawd, I sorry Cap'n.' Now their racism is saying, 'Is this nigger fucking with us or something?' They didn't know which foot to jump on. I never shot the other side because you can believe it would have been the other way. Since they didn't give you credit for cleverness, it allowed me a latitude I wouldn't have had.

—*excerpt from* What It Is, What It Was: The Black Film Explosion of the '70s in Words and Pictures *(Hyperion Books, 1998) edited by Gerald Martinez, Diana Martinez, and Andres Chavez*

MELVIN VAN PEEBLES (Composer): I have a sound in my head and the way a film should be. The way I see music, I treat it as one of the characters. That's how important it was to me. I treat it as one of my partners, one of my actors. You have to also remember that there was a racial situation and I had no one else to turn to. I had to do it myself. Truth of the matter is, I can't even read or write music. I just had to number everything on a piano and nobody ever taught me so I didn't think about it as intelligently as you're questioning me.

—*excerpt from "Sweetback in the Cosmos,"* Pop Matters, *October 15, 2014 by Matt Bauer*

HERMAN RAUCHER (Screenwriter): I wrote *Watermelon Man* as a screenplay first, as an original screenplay because I was involved in the black movement to some degree and I wanted to put my two cents in. This is '69, I think, and Columbia was afraid to make it without a black director, of whom there were not many. And they found Melvin Van Peebles in Europe somewhere. He'd done a film called *Story of a Three-Day Pass*. So Melvin was given the job of directing and it became, under his aegis, more of a black power film than I'd wanted. Melvin and I squared off a lot. I didn't really care for the film as much as I do other things I have done. I wrote the novelization afterwards, because, if I passed and didn't want to write it, Melvin could write it, and I thought it would just be too flammable. So in an odd way I wrote the novel in self defense. Melvin went on to do other things that were more to his liking and we never were great friends, but he was gifted and he was driven. God bless him, but I didn't want to work with him anymore.

I don't know how close you are to that film, but Estelle Parsons played Godfrey Cambridge's wife. It was about a white man who turns black because he's a bigot. And his wife was always liberal until he becomes black and is having trouble being black, and she becomes less supportive. And he says, "I thought you were liberal?" And she says, "I am...to a degree." And that's where I wanted to put my coin, because I thought that was the hypocrisy of many white people who were liberal to a degree, but they weren't when the chips were down. Now that was a big slice of ego for me to try and put that into a film. The line is in there, but I don't think the point I was trying to make ever surfaced. [Laughs.]

I was up for Black Writer of the Year. I had to call them and tell them I wasn't black, but I would tryout another time. [Laughs again.] And they said goodbye to me.

—excerpt from "Rediscovering Herman Raucher: The Life, Times, and Return of a 70s Pop Phenomenon," Cinedump, *Nov. 13, 2016, by Preston Fassel.*

CHUCK FRIES (Studio VP): Columbia Pictures had a very active program of pictures. In those days, we produced approximately twenty-five films per year at an overall annual production budget of $150 million, about the cost of one tentpole film in the twenty-first century. We were still producing $1.0/1. million films in England, under their subsidy plan, primarily for the foreign market with a limited American release to qualify them for the next theatrical package to sell to television. Each film had an American star to attract the theatrical audience and the network buyers. But the domestic production was robust also.

For example, I became enamored with a script submitted by former agent turned producer John Bennett. John had befriended a former ad executive named Herman Raucher who had taken a sabbatical and written about five spec scripts. One was entitled

Watermelon Man. It told the story of a white man who turns himself black to live in the African-American community to understand the discrimination of that time. The film's budget was only one million dollars and we assigned Melvin Van Peebles, one of the few available black directors, to take the reins. Melvin also composed the music. Godfrey Cambridge, a fine black actor, was signed to play the lead and through the use of special makeup, he played both a white and a black man in the film. His wife was played by Estelle Parsons. It was a good film and well received by the critics. Although a small film and not very profitable, I liked it because it was all mine.

—*excerpt from* Chuck Fries: Godfather of the Television Movie *(Monte Cristo Productions, 2010) by Chuck Fries.*

AN INTERVIEW WITH PRODUCER JOHN B. BENNETT

John Bennett started his entertainment career working as a talent agent for MCA and The Gersh Agency, where he represented a number of popular writers, directors, and actors. After leaving his position to produce films, he happened across an unfilmed screenplay by Herman Raucher, a screenwriter with several credits to his name. The script, then titled *The Night the Sun Went Down on Sleepy Hollow Lane* (terrible title!), was about a bigoted white man who wakes up one morning to discover he's somehow been transformed into a black man. Bennett optioned the screenplay and took it to Columbia, where it was made (as you obviously know if you're reading this book) and released as *Watermelon Man* in 1970.

Bennett later worked as an associate producer on Paul Bartel's *Private Parts*. He followed that working as a producer on the Delbert Mann-helmed NBC telefilm, *Francis Gary Powers: The True Story of the U-2 Spy Incident*. After that, he produced the 1979 Donald Sutherland-starrer *A Man, a Woman and a Bank*. He served as executive producer on the Gabe Kaplan/Bernadette Peters film, *Tulips*, before becoming a development executive at MGM/Orion. While in that position, Bennett produced the Chuck Norris actioner, *Forced Vengeance*, which is perhaps his best-known film.

I interviewed Bennett twice for this book. The conversation as it appears here is a combination of those interviews. In our first interview, which took place in 2020, Bennett shared some interesting anecdotes (which appear here). However, at the time he asked me not to publish them because he didn't want to offend Melvin Van Peebles. I agreed. When I interviewed Bennett again in 2022 (a few months after Van Peebles had died), the producer gave me permission to publish the stories.

Originally, I think Bennett had worried these stories might make Van Peebles sound arrogant and, perhaps, not all that talented (at that time). However, I believe these stories are important because they help us get a clearer picture of Van Peebles as an artist. Those of us who champion Van Peebles' work were already well aware that he had a tendency towards arrogance and could be self-serving. Those things were already accepted because those are among the traits that helped him achieve all the things he did. And if the studio truly believed Van Peebles was lacking in talent and had sought to fire him, then this is a testament to the fact that Van Peebles was an artist who was still learning his craft (and was *teaching himself* while doing the work). This story also reinforces what we already knew about Van Peebles—that he was facing (and clearing) a variety of hurdles, even if they were not necessarily (or were in addition to) the hurdles we were aware of. Even Bennett's assertion that Van Peebles wouldn't listen to anyone or take advice, be that good or bad, reinforces our preexisting image of an artist unwilling to compromise his creative vision.

When I spoke with Bennett, it was obvious that he genuinely liked Van Peebles and was one of his few white Hollywood supporters. And although his vocal inflections get lost in transcription, it was clear that Bennett wasn't judgmental of Van Peebles. If anything, he seemed amused by the director's antics and spoke of him the way one speaks of an old friend.

ANDREW J. RAUSCH: *How did you become involved with* Watermelon Man, *and what do you remember about the genesis of the project?*

JOHN B. BENNETT: I can't remember how I found the script, but I found it, and I read it, and I liked it. So I set about trying to put it together. I first went to a director named Jack Smight, who was a very well-known television director. Not a big name, a modest name. But he was very good. He had done a couple of features. He was a white guy, naturally. And we thought maybe Alan Alda could play the part. I got the script to Alda, and he read it and said he would do it. Then I took it around, and I took it to an executive that

I knew at Universal. He read it and he talked around the studio about it, and they turned it down. He said, "Listen, you've got to find a black director to do this because it's a controversial kind of story." And I said, "There aren't any!" So anyway, he said he knew Melvin, so he gave me Melvin's phone number. And I spoke to Melvin, who was in New York. I sent him the script and he read it. He said he liked it and he would do it. So I flew to New York and I met with him, and we agreed to work together on it.

So I went to Columbia, where I had worked before. I got it to Stanley Schneider, who was head of the studio. Subsequently, when he left the studio, it was his uncle who was the New York guy who made all the big decisions. He became a producer, and he was the producer on the famous Paramount picture *Three Days of the Condor*. He ended up being on the set and had a heart attack and died. And that was actually the only time I met Stanley Schneider—the time I went to New York and took Melvin in to meet him. We came out with a verbal agreement that if I could make it for a million dollars... He put a million dollars for it, and I was able to get a budget drawn up that convinced him to okay it.

So, we had a picture to make. And that was that.

AR: *Was that the first film you produced?*

JB: Yes, it was. I had been an agent for thirteen years. I had been an officer in the Army in Korea. I was Assistant Company Commander there, and then became a First Lieutenant. While I was there, I was offered a regular Army commission if I wanted to make the Army my career. I turned it down. I did not particularly care for the military. I was able to get out of Korea two months early to go to UCLA graduate school, which I did. I got my Master's Degree in Marketing, and I started making the rounds. I interviewed with McCann Erickson, NBC, and some others. And I got a job as an agent. I liked it, but I ultimately decided I wanted to try my way as a producer.

I was able to get this script set up, and *Watermelon Man* became my first picture. I even suggested that the studio bring in an experienced executive producer.

AR: *What do you remember about your executive producer, Leon Mirell?*

JB: He was a terrific guy, but he had absolutely nothing to do with the movie in any way other than the fact that he lent us his name, and he picked up fifty grand. The reason was that I had never produced anything.

AR: *Since you would go on to produce other films, I wondered, how was* Watermelon Man *as a first film? Did you learn a lot from that?*

JB: Yeah, I learned a lot. I found a mentor at Columbia Studio. A man named Chuck Fries. He was the second in command at the studio and the head of business affairs. He was also involved with everything that went on with the studio. I wasn't an experienced producer at all, so he took me under his wing. As a matter of fact, he just died about two months ago. He was ninety-three. Maybe about six years ago, he wrote an autobiography of himself. He executive produced or produced, ultimately, over one hundred "Movies of the Week." He basically invented the Movie of the Week concept. I became very close to him. I actually took a job working for his company for a while when he was an independent producer. And when he wrote his autobiography, he wrote a whole chapter about *Watermelon Man* and me.

I didn't find this out until we were in our eighties, but Chuck and me were both in the same fraternity when we were in college. He went to Ohio State and I went to UCLA, and we were both SAEs. At any rate, Chuck Fries was my mentor who helped me become a producer. I was forever grateful to him for that. And as I say, I ultimately worked with him for a while and we produced a Movie of the Week together, *The Francis Gary Powers Story*, which I had found. I also became friends with Frank Powers. He was the guy who flew the U2 spy plane that got shot down over Russia. He ultimately died flying a helicopter over Van Nuys. There was always a feeling that he had been murdered because he knew so much about the U2 spy plane incident. There was always that rumor. It was never proven. He was the same age as I was, and he had flown thirty-one thousand hours in the air. And the reason that he died is that was at 1,500 feet in his helicopter and he ran out of gas. The helicopter just dropped to the ground! And a guy with that kind of experience doesn't just run out of gas. And it turned out to be a good movie. It was a Movie of the Week because I was able to talk Delbert Mann, an Academy Award-winning director into doing it.

Anyway, what else do you want to talk about?

AR: *What do you remember about the first time you met Melvin Van Peebles? What was your first impression of him? Do you remember?*

JB: I liked him. I always liked him. I didn't have any contact with him, and hadn't for years, but I liked the guy. He was just who he was. He was pretty upfront with being arrogant, but that arrogance hides an insecurity complex. And it makes sense. He was insecure because he was black in a white man's world. He had a lot of balls to do what he did. He was a very courageous guy. So, in a lot of ways, I admire him a lot. He just wouldn't listen to anybody's suggestions on how to do something better. He just wanted to do things on his own, and he felt that he was a genius. And he wasn't. He was *close* to it. He was a very, very smart guy. He just wouldn't listen to anybody, and consequently, Peter Guber and I had to remake that picture in the editing room. After he turned in his cut, we went in and we literally remade the picture. It's not a great picture now, but it holds together. His cut was disastrous.

AR: *You told me your first viewing of Melvin's cut with Peter Guber was pretty memorable?*

JB: When we finished the screening he said, "Well, Bennett, it's too long. It's just sitting there. We can't release it like that." He said, "We've got to do something about that, don't we?" And I said, "Yes, we sure do." And that was it. We went to work on it. With the film editor. I picked the film editor. He was a guy that I knew quite well. Carl Kress was his name. He was a friend and a terrific film editor, and he did the best he could. He had done what Melvin told him to do. An editor doesn't make those decisions. The filmmaker does, and the editor executes them. But Carl Kress was a very good film editor and he went on to do many other things and eventually retired up in Bishop. Up in the high Sierra. He was a great guy. Listen, I was lucky enough to be around some great people in the film business. And those people I worked with, I had a lot of great feelings for.

But Peter Guber and I felt the picture was too long and dragged in some places, which is why we [recut] it. We took fourteen minutes out of the picture. When Melvin came back, he was livid. "You can't do that! Whitey fucked me!" And Peter said, "You'll never work again in this town if you go in and make waves." So Melvin went along with it, and we released the film fourteen minutes shorter.

AR: *What can you tell me about the original cut of* Watermelon Man*? What were some of the differences between that cut and the version that was released?*

JB: That's difficult to remember, but it was primarily that he let scenes play too long. He just wouldn't cut it right. He wasn't knowledgeable about it. So anyway, the cut came out as you saw it and it was good enough to release and let people see it.

AR: *So Melvin wasn't the director you had hoped he would be when you hired him?*

JB: Look, Melvin brought a lot of creativity to the movie, but he was arrogant. His arrogance really pissed Herman Raucher off. Raucher really did not like him at all. But Melvin didn't care whether he made enemies or not. He just didn't care. By the way, when he finished the picture, Columbia studio made it clear to me that they would never hire him again. He never knew that. He was out getting the money for his own movie and all that. And he really had very little contact with the studio.

I mean, when the picture opened in New York, I went back for the opening of the picture, but Melvin didn't come. It opened at the Murray Hill Theatre on 24th Street. That's where it opened, and it opened immediately after *Joe*, a picture that played for five weeks and set a record at the theater. And then *Watermelon Man* broke it. It played really well at Murray Hill, and then it opened at theater in Westwood, and I attended that opening.

Then, when they had the black Academy Awards the next year, they invited me to be the presenter of the director's award, which was quite an honor. You know, it's like the Academy Awards but it's for blacks only. So I got up there and made a short speech and announced the winner, and it turned out it was Martin Ritt who won the award. He was a great director. And he was not there, so I accepted the award for him.

But Melvin had nothing to do with the movie after it was finished.

AR: *Do you know why Melvin didn't attend the premiere of the movie? Was it because he was unhappy with the release cut?*

JB: He wasn't invited to watch it. I mean, we eventually showed it to him. And he, as I best remember, he didn't piss on it, but he was smart enough to realize that's the way the cookie crumbles and that was the way the picture was gonna go out. So he said, "Yeah, okay." I can't remember exactly what he said, but he didn't piss on it, and he also didn't say it was great. His ego wouldn't let him say that it was really improved. But he didn't piss on it, and he didn't say it was fantastic.

The studio had very little to do with him afterwards because they did not really respect his talents at that point. Even though he did a great job on certain things in the picture. He really did. The music, particularly. He's not without talent. It's just that he had a hard time in his lifetime marshaling his talent and equating it with his ego. And it was understandable. Here's a guy who came up on the other side of the tracks. He was a conductor of cable cars and he ends up writing a novel in Dutch and making a little movie in Paris. That's a fantastic accomplishment. You've got to give him his due. And he went on to have a terrific career in the commodities market as a seller of commodities. But he got to a point where the industry walked away from him. The little movie that he made [*Sweet Sweetback's Badasssss Song*] cost about $300,000, maybe $350[000]. And it obviously was not well-received in the industry because it was seen as being kind of an anti-white movie. I don't remember much about it. I think his son Mario was in it. And Mario has subsequently become a highly-respected director. And he still is. And as a matter of fact, he had a walk-on part in *Watermelon Man*. You have to look very closely, but he's there. He was just on the set one day and Melvin put him in the scene.

As a matter of fact, I don't know how well you remember the movie, but there's a scene at a stoplight where Godfrey is in the bus. It pulls up to a stoplight, and while he's waiting there, a little motorcycle pulls up alongside the bus. A guy is riding the motorcycle, and he's just stopped there. So we cut in close on the motorcycle. And then if you look in the credits, there's a credit to Indian motorcycles. And the reason for it is, they gave me two motorcycles to put that in the picture. [Laughs.] I gave Melvin one of them, and I kept one of them! So he had a motorcycle he got from the movie. I took pretty good care of Melvin. As I say, he never told me this, but he was really saving his money to put it into his own movie, which he ultimately financed on his own. He never put up a quarter. He never picked up a lunch tab. There's only one guy in the industry that I know of that was as tight as Melvin was, and that was one of the most famous actors of all time, and that was Cary Grant. He was the tightest person. He never ever picked up a lunch tab ever.

AR: *That's pretty nifty how you managed to get free motorcyles just by product placing them in the film.*

JB: They get a listing as well as three or four other products. I negotiated all of those myself. I got free milk delivered for a year. To my house. Two quarts every other day. Cottage cheese. I don't remember for sure, but I think it was the Adohr milk company. If you look at the movie's closing credits, there are four or five products credited. I'm the only one who did that. Nobody else had anything to do with any of that.

AR: *I wanted to ask you about some of the things that Melvin has said over the years. One of the statements that he always made was that he was hired and intentionally set up to fail.*

JB: That doesn't make sense and I'll tell you why. After the first day of shooting, the head of the studio, Bob Weitman, put a call into me. "Get your ass up here!" I went up to his office and he said, "Have you seen the dailies?" I said yes. He said, "You know, the guy can't direct." I said, "I know." He said, "Fire him." I said, "You'll never hear the end of it if you fire him. Never. You can't do it. You've got to bite the bullet." He thought about it and said, "You're right. Okay, we'll keep him on. Go do the best you can." That was the story. It wasn't that he was set up to fail. He just wasn't a very talented director. And subsequently, it was proven. The reason he was not a very good director is very simple: he wouldn't listen to anybody. He did exactly what he wanted, and that's that. Subsequently, Warners hired him to do a car race picture with Richard Pryor [*Greased Lightning*]. He filmed about two or three weeks of that, and they fired him. And they didn't fire him because he was black. The film had a black star! They fired him because he was an incompetent director.

The guy they got to replace him was Michael Shultz, who was a black man. He was a pretty good director, and I knew him. We tried to put something together at one time. You know, after *Watermelon Man* I became kind of known as the white guy who could work with a black guy. Michael Shultz was a very nice guy who was not arrogant. He directed a lot of television and did a couple of features.

But they threw Melvin off of that picture.

AR: *Another story that Melvin was fond of telling was that he had promised the studio that he would shoot both endings, but then tricked them and never shot the original. Is that accurate?*

JB: I have no memory of that at all. But the ending that was used was a much better ending. I think Peter and I just accepted the ending in the picture. We liked it. We thought it was good. And it was. It was a very functional, offbeat kind of ending.

You know, I probably would have made another picture with him if it had come to pass. If he had come to me and said, "Hey, I found a script and I think you ought to read it," I think the industry would have accepted me working with him. But by the time he got fired at Warners, he really became persona non grata at the studio. Because when you get fired from a studio, you'd better be really good. Because then you can weather the storm. But he had been up to bat twice with studio pictures, and the second picture... They didn't say good things about him at the studio. And if somebody from Fox had called and said, "We had a meeting with Melvin yesterday and he's got a terrific idea," they'd have said, "Don't hire him!" That's the first thing the studio would have said. His arrogance would have carried through. But Melvin was so resilient that he was able to find another job for himself outside the movie business that paid very good dividends. He became a commodities broker. And he was very good at it. And he made money at it.

AR: *I wanted to ask you about the soundtrack, which was, of course, composed by Melvin. It's an odd, unique soundtrack. Making music was another thing Melvin taught himself to do, which is fascinating. What are your thoughts on the soundtrack?*

JB: It was a good soundtrack. He did a good job. He was a better songwriter than he was a film director. He was very accomplished with that. There were two songs he used in it that I remember were pretty well known at that time. And we bought them. There was a usual fee paid for songs at that time. I think it was five hundred dollars you paid to use a song in a movie. I think we bought the rights to a couple songs. But he did a good job with the soundtrack. He really did.

AR: *One interesting and extremely important thing Melvin did on this film was that he insisted on having black crew members because there really weren't any black crew members working at the time. What do you remember about that? How did that go over with the studio?*

JB: The studio loved that. They were all for it. We hired seven people. Six of them were black and one was Asian. They became assistants and would follow the film editor or around, or follow the cameraman, or follow the producer, or the director, and so forth. That was very functional and was the first time it had been done at a studio. It was very well-received, and a couple of the people went on to good jobs in the entertainment business. I know my own assistant ultimately became an agent, and he was pretty good at that.

I'll tell you a story. My assistant shadowed me everywhere. He'd sit in my office, sit in on my phone calls, go to my meetings. It was a great educational experience and I retained a friendship with him for many, many years. Every day at ten till eight, before we would start shooting, Melvin and I would meet and go over what was going to be filmed that day. And my assistant was always there standing by my side, listening.

Melvin loved to tell me about his sexual conquests. And one Monday morning, we met at ten minutes till eight. He said, "Bennett, I gotta tell you who I fucked yesterday. I was in Griffith Park, and I ran into her, and I gave her a spiel, and I fucked her right away." Her name was Sue Lyon and she was very, very famous, and starred in *Lolita*. He said, "I fucked her *uphill*! I got her in Griffith Park and I fucked her on a hill." Then he said, "Okay, I better go set this scene up." He left, and the assistant came over and put his arm around my neck. He leaned in close and he said, "I fucked her on Saturday!" And I never told Melvin because Melvin would have just blown his own brains out on that one! [Laughs.]

Melvin was really a scavenger with women. He was very aggressive with women. I had two or three experiences with him when I was in New York that were just embarrassing. [Chuckles.] I remember we were walking down Fifth Avenue and he passed a good-looking woman. He said, "Just a minute." He turned around and walked up to her and he tapped her on the shoulder. He said, "Would you like to fuck?" I mean, it's not what you call classy.

But anyway... That program, I'm sure, was picked up at the other studios, and that was all Melvin's idea. It was a terrific idea, and I jumped on it. I was the one who had to put it into effect. And it worked quite well.

AR: *Whenever Herman Raucher discusses* Watermelon Man *in an interview, he's always tactful and never says anything bad, but you always get a very clear sense that he didn't care for the film.*

JB: Herman did not like Melvin, but he also doesn't like Hollywood. But he's tactful. He's a very bright guy and a really great writer. He had his reasons for not caring for Melvin, and I'm sure that colored his liking or disliking of the movie. But that script is about 90-percent Raucher's. The ending isn't, but most of it is. It was a long time ago. Herman is a very independent guy himself. I just always thought the world of him. He never really forgave me, I think, for getting along with Melvin. But listen, I had to be diplomatic. That's what a producer does; he's got to be a diplomat.

AR: *Let's talk about Godfrey Cambridge. He was immensely talented. What do you remember about working with him?*

JB: He's a fabulous guy. He's a very funny, very talented actor. I'm the one who got the script to him. He read it and said he would do it. He actually, very early on, did not like Melvin. It didn't start until the shooting began. But by the end of the first week, he didn't like Melvin. And that was very unlike him. And the reason was that Melvin was the boss, as he should have been, but he wouldn't consult with Godfrey. He would tell Godfrey how he wanted him to play a scene. He did a line reading. Godfrey was a pretty experienced actor by the time, and that offended him. He didn't appreciate that. So they just didn't get along. Godfrey said to me once, "Bennett, we've got to figure out who the head nigger in charge is." [Laughs.] Godfrey needed a psychiatrist to get by. He had a lot of conflicts. Part of his contract said he could leave at eleven o'clock each day during shooting. He had one hour to go to his dressing room and get on the phone and talk to his psychiatrist. So, he would have a shrink meeting every day of shooting for one hour. From eleven to twelve. That's a rarity, but he had to have it. He just had a lot of complexes. He was such a nice man. He meant well, and he was a *good* actor. He gave a good performance.

As a matter of fact, Melvin wasn't even involved with making Godfrey's make-up. He was in New York, and we had to make Godfrey look white. I got Ron Berkeley, who was Richard Burton's make-up man, and I convinced the studio to give us a day in the make-up office to experiment with make-up. Melvin wasn't there. It was just Godfrey, Ron Berkeley, and me, and we spent the whole day in the make-up room putting on different make-ups, trying to make Godfrey look white. And if you saw the picture, he doesn't look white! He looks Mexican! [Laughs.] We could never get it light enough because Godfrey's skin was so dark. And it would come through a sort of Latino color. Any rate, that was great fun. The three of us had fun doing it and Ron Berkeley was a great guy. They paid him five hundred dollars for the day, but he was the top make-up man in the business. To come in and do that was kind of fun for him. So, we did the best we could, and Melvin, of course, accepted it. There was nothing he could do about it, because we'd already done it.

You know, I got to know Godfrey really well. He was really a nice man. His main problem was that he tended to over-eat. Before he would go work on a picture or go off on tour, he would go on a crash diet, and he'd lose thirty or forty pounds in the space of two or three months. He went to Sweden to do his act. As he told me, "You know, I would go to parties in Sweden and I'd be the only black person there." He said, "This woman came up to me and said, 'We just really love you being here. We just love black people. We're not prejudiced against anybody. Of course, there are the Laplanders, who are all in the North, and they're all shiftless and on welfare.'" Godfrey thought that was interesting. The Swedes have their prejudices; it's not blacks, it's the Laplanders who lived up there in the snow country. Godfrey put that into his act. I thought it was very funny and very telling about the fact that people are prejudiced all over. But in some places there aren't any blacks to be prejudiced against, so they find their own people to be prejudiced against.

But Godfrey was a really nice man. He just didn't like Melvin.

AR: *When we spoke before, you were telling me about an incident between Godfrey and Melvin at the end of the shoot. Now that we're doing the actual interview, could you tell me that story on the record?*

JB: It's kind of a tradition in the business that the director would give a little present to his lead. It isn't always done. Maybe it isn't even often done. But Melvin gave a Zippo lighter to Godfrey as a sort of going away present. Godfrey was very angry at Melvin, so he just took the lighter and threw it as far as he could throw it. He did not want any gift from Melvin. It's a shame, too, because it's entirely possible that if Melvin had treated Godfrey a little better... Godfrey would not say good things about Melvin in public. He just wouldn't.

AR: *How did Melvin react to Godfrey throwing the lighter?*

JB: I can't remember. I think he just said, "Ah, fuck it." I know this much, he didn't walk over there and ask him, "Why'd you do that?" Because he knew why he did it. [Laughs.]

AR: *What were some of the differences between Herman Raucher's original script and what made it into the film? I know the ending was different.*

JB: Well, the ending was very different. Actually, Melvin did make changes in the script himself, and that offended Raucher. Melvin just did whatever he wanted with the script. But Melvin is not known for his tact. He could have gotten Herman involved in every one line change, but he would just do it. And his feelings were that he was the expert on the black experience, and he was right. He was. I don't know if Raucher ever bought the ending. But it's the filmmaker's right to change a script the way he feels it would be come off. Look, the script came off as a terrific script. It really did. For a low-budget film.

AR: *I've been trying to get a hold of a shooting script.*

JB: I have one somewhere out in the garage, but there's a lot of stuff to dig through out there. I do have the book, though. Have you seen the book?

AR: *Yes, I have. I bought it hoping it had Raucher's original ending because I was curious to see that.*

JB: That's because the book wasn't written until after the movie was finished. That's a rarity because usually movies are made from books. But this was an original screenplay. The fact is, Herman was not enamored with Melvin. When the publisher wanted the book written, they went to Melvin. And actually, Herman didn't want to write the book. But when he found out that if he didn't write it, Melvin was gonna write it, he said, "No way!" So he got paid two thousand dollars to write the book.

AJR: *The film was originally titled* The Night the Sun Went Down on Sleepy Hollow Lane. *At what point in the production was the title changed, and whose idea was that?*

JB: You know, I don't remember. The title came as the picture was in production. The script that we had as a shooting script had that other title on it. I can't tell you where "Watermelon Man" came up, and I don't remember who created the title. It very well could have been Melvin.

AR: Watermelon Man *is certainly a snazzier title. Raucher's original title doesn't really roll off the tongue.*

JB: No, it doesn't. *Watermelon Man* is a good title. And it's lived because, as you might remember from the cover of the novel, which is a softcover, it's got a watermelon and it's sort of got a funny-looking American flag on the watermelon. Then below it's got a picture from one of the ads, I guess.

So, I don't know when the title came up, but it was somewhere during the production. Because when we went into post-production, I think we had the new title.

AR: *Godfrey Cambridge was pretty outspoken about hating the new title because he felt it was demeaning to black people, so he said he wouldn't promote the film.*

JB: I don't remember that. The only thing that I really remember is that he hated the director. He did not like the director at all.

Melvin was a funny guy. I don't wanna put him down, particularly now that he's gone, but he was arrogant, which concealed an inferiority complex.

AR: *You guys also cast Estelle Parsons. What do you remember about her?*

JB: She was absolutely terrific in the movie. And an extremely nice person. I ran into her a couple times later in New York on my trips. I never got a chance to use her again. She worked after that. That movie did her career a bit of good. It was helpful to her to become more well known in the industry. But *Watermelon Man* helped her career. Melvin had heard of her from New York. I didn't know who she was. Melvin was instrumental in casting her. I was instrumental in casting Godfrey.

AR: *Musician Paul Williams has a very small cameo in the film. What do you remember about him?*

JB: That was Melvin that put him in that part. He'd somehow met him. Paul Williams was into music, and Melvin was into music. He put him in that, and the guy was nice in it. He did fine. I never got to know him real well. But he went on to do interesting things in his life.

I'll tell you, Melvin and I worked pretty good on casting. We didn't have a lot of arguments, Melvin and I. We didn't fight. I took care of my responsibilities, like the budget and seeing that things were in the right place at the right time. The things that a producer does to try to make things a little easier on the director.

AR: *Let's talk about Mantan Moreland. He's an interesting actor, and he's also got a small role in there.*

JB: Oh, that was all Melvin. He found him, and he cast him in the role. He nursed him through it, because the guy couldn't remember a line. He helped him through whatever he had to say. This was one of the last things that Moreland did. There were two or three people who had small roles in that picture that Melvin dug up out of the woodwork. Mantan Moreland was one.

AR: *Do you have any memories regarding the release of the film?*

JB: I was divorced from my first wife, and I had a girlfriend who was white and she was an American Airlines stewardess. I remember when *Watermelon Man* opened, it played in the Detroit Theater in Detroit, which was the largest theater outside of Radio City Music Hall. It had 4,995 seats. And she had a layover with a white stewardess partner, and they decided to go see *Watermelon Man* because she was my girlfriend. I mean, we were pretty hot and heavy at that time. She said she went into the theater and there wasn't an empty seat. It was 4,995 black people in there. And she said it was a little dicey for her.

I have a lot of good memories about that movie. And I have a lot of good memories about Melvin.

AR: *Have you been surprised by the continued popularity of* Watermelon Man*? It's had a Blu-ray release and it's going to become a Criterion film this year.*

JB: I have been surprised. I was invited to a screening of it about two years ago. Somebody had a screening at a theater. I went to it and I took my wife and one of my daughters. There were maybe a hundred people there. And I didn't know why they screened it, but they did.

You know, I had some talks right before the pandemic about doing a remake of *Watermelon Man* with a woman playing the role. A woman named Leslie Jones who is on *Saturday Night Live*.

She's about a six-foot-one-inch fifty-year-old very darkly complected black lady who is quite funny and quite a good actress. Her agent called me and said she wanted to do a remake and play the Godfrey Cambridge part. And I said I thought that was a great idea. I had several conversations with him. I'm not sure why it never went further. Maybe it's because of the pandemic and still can happen.

I said I didn't want to produce it. I would be the executive producer and give them any help that I could. I would talk to Raucher about it and get any help he wished to give. At any rate, nothing came of it. It's not impossible. I can resurrect it if I made the right phone call to the studio. It certainly might be worth pursuing.

WATERMELON TALK: OBSERVATIONS ON THE FILM

Today, it's impossible to imagine any other actor playing the role of Jeff Gerber. And this is not just because audiences have been watching him play this role for more than fifty years. In short, Godfrey Cambridge owns this role and plays it in a way no one else could have. That's not to say no one else could have been good in the part, but Cambridge makes it his own.

While most white audiences at the time didn't get the joke or the subtext of the film, Melvin Van Peebles (with a script by white screenwriter Herman Raucher) inverted the tradition of blackface performance. In Van Peebles' mind, the joke of white men in blackface (a one-note joke he did not find humorous) was that the white actor would portray broad stereotypes of black people. So, the white men behaved "normally" before becoming black and then playing goofy. In *Watermelon Man*, Van Peebles does the opposite; Cambridge's Jeff Gerber is a broad stereotype who acts absurdly. It's only when Gerber becomes black that he begins to behave normally. So, the joke is on the white audience.

One of the reasons Van Peebles was able to do this so openly in 1970 is because he, in a film that is otherwise anything but subtle in its messaging, did this one thing somewhat subtly. (Subtle, at least for the white audience; it seems likely that the black audience knew exactly what was happening.) The key to this was Van Peebles' casting of Godfrey Cambridge. Cambridge was a black comic who had been a favorite of white audiences for years by this point. As such, Cambridge had been forced, at least to some degree, to become a version of himself deemed palatable for white people in the 1960s. He became the "safe" black performer who "acted white." Cambridge was so "safe" and readily embraced by white audiences that he made Sidney Poitier look like Huey Newton in contrast. And maybe this persona wasn't manufactured. Because he'd spent much of his life attending predominantly white schools and living in predominantly white locations, perhaps Cambridge's persona was, in fact, the real Cambridge. While Van Peebles himself had spent a few years surrounded by European whites, he didn't compromise or alter his behavior to please them. So, the way Cambridge behaved (at least publicly) and was accepted by whites wasn't lost upon Van Peebles. (Example: After making *Watermelon Man*, Cambridge said his main takeaway from the film was, "Black is beautiful, but so is white." It's hard to imagine Van Peebles saying this.) So, Van Peebles used the comic/actor as a sort of Trojan horse to make white audiences comfortable to a degree where the filmmaker's messaging would slip by largely unnoticed. Beyond Van Peebles using Cambridge's persona to distract the audience, who could have been better to cast in a role in which a black actor acts like a white man than Cambridge, a black performer who had spent much of his own life doing just that?

Another reason Cambridge was perfectly cast is that his comedic timing is spot-on. His exaggeratedly goofy white man laugh is so perfectly over-the-top one can't help but laugh right along with him.

Cambridge's Jeff Gerber first exhibits a goofy intensity as he is shown working out. During these scenes, Van Peebles hilariously alternates between shots of Gerber lying in a tanning bed and Althea toasting white bread in the toaster. In the role, Cambridge conveys smugness while simultaneously acting exaggeratedly goofy. One of the best examples of Jeff Gerber's white man weirdness is the scene where he foot races a bus. This is absurd. I doubt there are people out there who race city buses while wearing suits, but I think it's relatively safe to assume that if such a person does exist, he's a white guy. Since screenwriter Herman Raucher's original intentions for the film's messaging were different from Van Peebles', it's unclear exactly what his original purpose for writing the bus-chasing scenes was. Van Peebles no doubt embraced these silly scenes because they worked perfectly in helping him achieve the inverted blackface "silly when white" statement he wanted to make.

The film (and Cambridge) goes out of its way to make sure we know that white Jeff is an uncool goofball. (Like many things in the film, the depiction of white Jeff as a cornball is not particularly subtle.) He's a guy who sports ugly pajamas, doesn't like sex, acts like a buffoon whenever possible, and is so whiny and annoying that hardly anyone likes him or wants to be around him. White Jeff is a guy who is tolerated by the people around him. Also interesting is the fact that Jeff isn't a character we can empathize with until after his transformation; not that we, the audience, have ever changed colors, but black Jeff behaves (somewhat) like an actual human being. In addition, Cambridge speaks in a more "normal" voice after becoming black Jeff.

Cambridge and Van Peebles exaggerate the level of Gerber's obnoxious open bigotry (in front of black characters like the coffee shop worker and the bus driver), but sadly, probably not by much. But there is a reason Van Peebles does this. By amplifying Jeff's bad behavior, the filmmaker can make its inappropriateness more apparent to a white audience who, at the time, was largely apathetic to the point of probably not even noticing when it was happening around them.

Something else that's key in these scenes involving Gerber's blatantly bad behavior in front of the black coffee shop worker is the casting of Mantan Moreland. Van Peebles' casting of Moreland was sheer brilliance. While still conveying Gerber's general asshole-ishness the way screenwriter Raucher had intended, Van Peebles added another layer of messaging. Moreland, like Cambridge, and probably even more so, had made a career of yukking it up in a safe, easily digestible manner for white audiences. When Gerber becomes black, Moreland's character drops his facade. The character, like Moreland himself, had been forced to play nice in front of his white audience. But in this scene and with this casting, Van Peebles allows Moreland to do publicly what he had likely always wanted to do, which was to show everyone that he was someone else—someone *real*—after his white audience is gone. The character is visibly exhausted from the burden of being forced to wear a metaphorical mask. While this joke got a laugh from the knowing black audience, it showed white people that black performers (like Moreland) were simply putting on a happy, friendly face for them and, in reality, probably didn't care for the white onlookers any more than the white onlookers cared about them.

It's a testament to Van Peebles' genius that he was able to take the preexisting scenes written by Raucher and, with a few tweaks, completely change their meaning while adding additional messaging and nuance. Whatever then-novice filmmaker Van Peebles may have lacked in technical proficiency, he was doing something here that no one else was doing (or *had* to do), and he was doing it *well*.

If we're truly being honest, Van Peebles was handed a half-assedly funny script with which to work. This isn't to say the film isn't funny. It's funny because the one-note joke around which it's constructed is funny (and intriguing). But many of the individual jokes fall flat; Jeff chasing buses and taking a bath in milk while chanting "Ooga-booga-dooga-doo!" are cringe-inducing. *Watermelon Man* is similar to an episode of *Twilight Zone* in that its entire story hangs on its "twist." On the classic TV show, most of the episode serves only as a means to get us to the twist at the end of the story. The scenes that precede the twist are well done and equally compelling in many episodes. However, there are more than a few episodes where the scenes leading up to the twist feel like filler. *Watermelon Man* is similar, although, in Van Peebles' film, the twist is delivered at the beginning of the story. Then much of what follows Jeff's revelation feels like filler rounding out the film's running time. (Too much time is given to Jeff in a plaster of Paris head or his attacking the delivery man.) In this regard, *Watermelon Man* is a mediocre-to-upper-level *Twilight Zone* episode in which some of the other stuff works, and some doesn't. But like the very best episodes, *Watermelon Man* contains poignant social commentary. Van Peebles' film shares another trait with many *Twilight Zone* episodes in that it doesn't provide a pat explanation as to *why* Jeff turns black. There are some silly suggestions—nonsense about sunlamps and soy sauce—but no *real* explanation.

An interesting thing about the film is Althea's almost instant change in how she addresses her husband. While she still cracks dumb jokes and seems largely unaffected for an extended period, her wording changes almost immediately. After applying cream to

Jeff's face, Althea says, "I don't think any intelligent negro expects it to be immediate." She sounds condescending and superior while identifying Jeff as an "other." Note that Althea replaces the word "person (which she would have used if Jeff were still white) with "negro" in the sentence. This tells us that "liberal" Althea references black people differently than she does whites. So, despite trying her best to pretend she's color blind, the way Althea speaks about black people shows us otherwise. In addition to all this, she also labels him "militant."

Equally telling is Jeff's response: "I'm not militant. I'm white. I expect it to be immediate." This response not only displays Jeff's entitlement as a white man but also tells us that these white suburbanites view black people who desire the same things they *expect*—equality if you will—as being *militant*. That right-wing catchphrase was used to frighten white people of the time (there are similar dog whistle phrases used today) into believing that black people were/are naturally violent. It also served to de-legitimize the complaints and desires of the black community.

White Jeff makes several offhand remarks about black people rioting. He makes it clear that he believes the rioters are simply stirring up shit and overreacting (presumably for the sake of doing so). But when black Jeff cynically (and correctly) predicts the impending racism directed towards him and his family, it is clear that he has known all along (and ignored) the fact that black people's complaints were valid and that they routinely faced hate and discrimination from people like Jeff and his neighbors.

Althea also represents the white people who are fully aware that their racism is terrible but still make excuses for it ("it's the way I was raised" or "the Confederate flag is part of my heritage"). Althea says, "I'm ashamed of myself," but then follows that up by saying, "But I can't help it."

The scene in which black Jeff is attacked and stopped by the police for chasing the bus isn't particularly subtle, but it is accurate. Black Jeff is treated like a criminal for doing the same things white Jeff has been doing all along without trouble. This problem persists today with people like "Barbecue Becky" and "Pool Patty" (both real) calling the police to report black people doing mundane things. An even bleaker real-life example is Ahmaud Arbery, the Georgia black man murdered by white men in 2020 simply for jogging through the wrong neighborhood.

The film also offers examples of the burden black people are forced to shoulder when they and their actions are viewed as being representative of their entire race. When Jeff's boss informs him that he's called the NAACP to tell them he's employed a black man, he advises Jeff, "Don't let them down!" In another instance, a title card appears on the screen (one of several), saying, "Be a credit to your race!" A third example is when Althea warns black Jeff not to kill the delivery man because she feels black people in the city have enough problems as it is.

Another of the film's title cards says, "You get use to the smell... and there's a lot to be grateful for..." The literal meaning of this refers to working at the dump, but at its heart, it's a metaphor about the plight of black America, with the white man saying, "I know your lack of equality sucks, but hang in there, and you'll get used to it. You have a lot to be grateful for."

The film provides two more examples of the "black is normal" whiteface motif. The first is when Jeff meets the black doctor. The white doctor he's been seeing has consistently been an absolute idiot, but the black doctor behaves like an actual person. Another (possibly unintended) example is when Jeff and Althea's neighbors come into their home to buy them out of the neighborhood. The white mob is led by a dumb-acting schlub (who looks kind of like Vincent Pastore from *The Sopranos*) who is by far and away the worst actor in the film. In fact, he's the only bad actor in the movie. He speaks in a mumbly monotone manner, and his poor "acting" adds to the effect; everything about this character screams stupidity.

Just after Jeff has accepted that he is a black man and has resigned himself to live as such, Melvin Van Peebles shows up in a dialogue-less cameo as a man stenciling Jeff's name on his office door. I sincerely doubt that Van Peebles intended his appearance to have such a meaning, but the appearance could be seen as Van Peebles endorsing Jeff's decision to embrace his blackness. Since Van Peebles is the creator pulling the strings, one could take this further and label him as a god endorsing Jeff's choice. Also interesting is the fact that the soundtrack becomes much more funky and upbeat after Jeff embraces his newfound blackness.

It should be noted that black Jeff establishes his own business. Rather than allowing himself to be defeated by a system hellbent on holding him down, Jeff, like Van Peebles himself, is pushing through and creating his own opportunities. Doing so (as stated in the book's introduction) is revolutionary; perhaps as revolutionary as Jeff training to fight his oppressor at the close of the film.

"COLUMN ITEMS" (FROM THE ORIGINAL FILM PRESSKIT)

These handy factoids were included in the original film presskit so newspapers or magazines that were writing pieces about the film would have extra details they could include. Some of these items aren't all that interesting, but there are at least some fascinating elements in each "column item" (presented here just as they appeared in the presskit). All of the inclusions in the presskit help to paint a picture of the way the studio was marketing the picture. Note how much of the emphasis in these column items put on the fact that Watermelon Man *was filmed "in color."*

Estelle Parsons, who won an Academy Award for her performance in her first film, *Bonnie and Clyde*, currently stars with Godfrey Cambridge in Columbia Pictures' *Watermelon Man*, a satiric comedy in color about a white who wakes up one morning to find he has turned black. She plays Cambridge's suburbanite wife.

Miss Parsons finds the principal difference between stage and screen is the difference between acting and performing. "In motion pictures, what you do is naturalistic, whereas on stage you're performing," she says. "In motion pictures you don't perform, you just act like a person."

When Godfrey Cambridge made Columbia Pictures' *Watermelon Man*, in color, in which he plays a white man who turns black, he said to Estelle Parsons, who also stars as his wife, "White, black, when I look in the mirror I still see ME!"

Melvin Van Peebles, the black director of Columbia Pictures' *Watermelon Man*, starring Godfrey Cambridge and Estelle Parsons in color, is the M.V. Peebles who records for Herb Alpert's A&M Records as Brer Soul. Van Peebles also wrote the music for *Watermelon Man*.

Black comedian-actor Mantan Moreland chalked up his 310th film when he appeared in an important supporting role in Columbia Pictures' *Watermelon Man*, in color. Godfrey Cambridge and Estelle Parsons are starred in the unusual comedy, story of a suburbanite who wakes up one morning to discover he has turned black.

Kim Kimberly, a sexpot from Australia who makes her film bow in Columbia Pictures' *Watermelon Man*, starring Godfrey Cambridge and Estelle Parsons in color, is a Kim Novak lookalike. The actress also is built along Kim's voluptuous proportions: Kay's vital statistics: 38-22-36.

"BLACK AND WHITE COMEDY IN COLOR" (FROM THE ORIGINAL FILM PRESSKIT)

This was a pre-prepared article supplied by Columbia Pictures in the original film presskit for newspapers to run in promoting the film. The newspaper could simply plug in the name of the local movie house and then slap it in their next issue. Again, note the emphasis Columbia placed on the fact that the film was "in color."

In Columbia Pictures's *Watermelon Man*, at the [insert name] Theatre in color, black comedian Godfrey Cambridge plays a brash white suburbanite who, one morning, discovers he has turned black. Estelle Parsons, Academy Award winner for her performance in *Bonnie and Clyde*, also stars as Cambridge's wife.

"The most difficult part of playing this white character was enduring the makeup that had to be applied every day," Cambridge said. Cambridge had to sit in the studio makeup department every day for a minimum of two hours while the cosmetics that transform him into a white person were applied. And, at the end of each shooting day, he would wearily plop down into the same chair to be returned to his natural color.

Veteran Columbia makeup man Ben Lane handled the transformations. For weeks prior to the start of shooting, Lane experimented on Godfrey with different greases, oils and paints. The final makeup blend turned out to be an orange tone which subdued Cambridge's naturally dark pigmentation sufficiently to permit the application of makeup that would result in his looking white. In addition to the "white" makeup, Cambridge also wears a wig of medium brown hair and matching eyebrows.

Even more difficult for Cambridge than the physical transformation were the mental gymnastics the actor had to go through to change from a black actor to a white character and back to his original identity,

In spite of Cambridge's minor complaints about enduring the discomfort of the makeup, he was quite enthusiastic about the film, declaring: "A black doing a role like the one I just played could do more for settling racial unrest than a thousand promises and lectures. In this picture we all, both black and white, take a good long look at ourselves. There's nothing better in the world than laughing at yourself. And when you think that I can play a white man one moment and like it, then turn around and be myself and like it, it's wild."

Watermelon Man was produced by John B. Bennett and directed by Melvin Van Peebles from Herman Raucher's screenplay. Leon Mirell was executive producer; Van Peebles also wrote the music for the Bennett-Mirell-Van Peebles Production.

TRUE COLORS: ON THE WATERMELON MAN SOUNDTRACK

by Michael A. Gonzales

The 1970 film *Watermelon Man*, written by Oscar nominated scribe Herman Raucher (*Summer of '42*) and directed by then-newcomer Melvin Van Peebles, was speculative fiction cinema, a "what if" scenario that would've fit perfectly as a vintage *Twilight Zone* episode or a short story in Harlan Ellison's *Dangerous Visions* collection. A satire on race and racism as well as the boundaries and patience of so-called liberals when faced with a dilemma that demands action over rhetoric, *Watermelon Man* followed the misadventures of a bigoted white man who turned "colored" in his sleep and stayed black forever.

The lead was played with gusto by actor and stand-up comic Godfrey Cambridge, whose *Cotton Comes to Harlem* was released that same year. He portrayed the boorish insurance executive Jeff Gerber who had a wonderful upper-middle-class existence, a Norman Rockwell kind of life complete with lovely wife Althea (Estelle Parsons) and two kids. One night, after a few too many incidents of harassing Negroes in public places and off-colored jokes at home, Gerber transformed into a Negro and spends the rest of the film proving he hasn't stolen anything or raped anyone.

Raucher wrote the original script as a broad farce, a literally "it was all a dream" film that would end in laughs, but director Melvin Van Peebles had other plans. The final product was funny, strange, disturbing and a "cinematic howl of rage," as *AV Club* critic Nathan Rabin dubbed it. It was also an absurd, Kafkaesque nightmare that, I'm sure, caused a few bad dreams itself.

Years back, I first saw *Watermelon Man* on the ABC late movie one Saturday night. There were a few race-based films the network showed during that period including *Guess Who's Coming to Dinner*, *The Skin Game* and *The Liberation of L.B. Jones*. Then again, with its shifts in tone, lighting choices and a strange soundtrack that sounded like nothing else in American films, *Watermelon Man* was the weirdest.

At the time I had no idea that Van Peebles was a soul brother from Chicago who had started making films while living as an expat in France from the late-50s to the mid-60s. Taking auteurism to the next level, Van Peebles was also the man behind the music. "I got into songs sideways, through the music that I needed for my films," he later told writer Bruce Pollock for the book *In Their Own Words* (Collier Books, 1975). "When I did my first short film (*Three Pickup Men for Herrick*) I needed music and couldn't afford to pay anyone, so I had a kazoo and I hummed my soundtrack. That was 1957. I got into it parallel with my other activities."

For better or worse, Van Peebles scored all of his own films including his pioneering indie picture *Sweet Sweetback's Baadasssss Song*, which came out a year after *Watermelon Man*. However, while Sweetback had a more accessible soundtrack featuring then-emerging funk band Earth, Wind & Fire, the *Watermelon Man* music incorporated many genres including ragtime, vaudeville and circus music. One of my favorite musical moments was when Gerber is going through his metamorphosis and the audience sees the reflection of flames on the same walls where there are pictures of their ivory-skinned elders, while the music was a weird jazz number.

"I remember when I first saw *Watermelon Man*," musician Paula Henderson, who played in Van Peebles' group Laxative, said. "I liked the movie, but I really loved the music, because it was so strange. Many people don't know about him as a musician, though. His music is under the radar." Melvin's bugged poetry and vocal stylings were inspired by Oscar Brown Jr. and the Last Poets while his songs influenced Gil Scott-Heron as well as more than a few hip-hop kids digging through the crates. Van Peebles' songs have been sampled by MF Doom ("Deep Fried Frenz"), Main Source ("The Man Tries Running His Usual Game but Sweetback Jones Is So Strong He..."/"Live at the Barbecue"), and Eric B. and Rakim ("Come on Feet Do Your Thing"/"Kick Along").

While *Sweetback*'s music helped create the sonic template for the Blaxploitation soundtracks of that era, the *Watermelon* music had more in common with Nino Rota's more upbeat scores mixed with minstrel shuffles, frantic free-jazz piano and crazy rockabilly. Interesting enough, while there's obviously a band playing these songs, the only musician listed in the liner notes was Ry Cooder on slide guitar. The music is steeped in the kind of sinister Americana that Beach Boy genius Brian Wilson was attempting to create on *Smile*, the 1966 project he abandoned a few years later.

As a kid growing up in the Windy City, Melvin was, in stark contrast to his playa playa persona, a nerdy bookworm who preferred reading, visiting museums and studying at the Chicago Arts Institute. "My mother asked why I didn't go outside and play, and I told her, 'Because the game is always kick Melvin's ass.' By the time I was ten, I'd seen nine people killed," he told me in 2014. As described in the novels of Richard Wright and Nelson Algren, the Chicago Streets of Peebles' (the Van insert in his name was added years later) youth were wild, loose and mean. The bad boys Peebles knew were, "the unknown guys who got wiped out. Guys you've never heard of, but I knew them."

In his autobiographical novel *A Bear for the FBI*, published in the states in 1968, he described being a young black boy growing up in Chicago. The "sharpness of being a negro . . . wears off and you get used to it just as if you have a wooden leg, or one eye and you don't notice it until you come to a high curb." For Van Peebles, that curb was when his parents moved to the suburbs. "There were fifty-three black kids out of three thousand. The kids' fathers were mailmen, Pullman porters or dentists."

However, while his classmates were enjoying after-school programs or hanging around the malt shop, Melvin journeyed into the city every afternoon to work with his father. Pops Peebles used to also take young Melvin around with him on various adventures through those Bronzeville blocks.

"If my mother protested, my father would just say, 'The boy's got to learn.' It was like I lived in two different worlds." Moreover, what he learned would stay with him always. "My father's shop was across the street from a spot called Gold's Bar and I used to hear all the music coming out of there. One day, I bought one of those records on 78 and my mother had a fit. The poor lady was trying to raise me one way and here I am listening to what she thought of as 'nigger music.'"

With a preference for Leadbelly, Blind Lemon Jefferson and Big Bill Broozy, the music still inspires him. "Blues was about the whole spectrum of life," Van Peebles says. "Work, love and life; it wasn't protest music, just life music." That blues aesthetic could be seen in his films and heard in the music he continued to make for the next few decades.

"When I first told Columbia Pictures I was going to do the music to *Watermelon Man* they almost had a heart attack," Van Peebles said. "But, I was in the union and it was in my contract that I could hire who I wanted, so I hired myself." With that slick move, Van Peebles joined the small group of black men who made Hollywood soundtracks: Duke Ellington and Quincy Jones.

Considering the bizarre musical cues in the film that include free jazz piano when the family was watching civil rights protests on television, sexy burlesque bops when the wife walks across the room, I'm sure some executives were baffled. In addition, the soundtrack was often as obnoxious as the main character and pounding in when least expected.

Though far from a traditional theme song, the track "Love, That's America" plays throughout the film, adding sonic blow with its patriotic July fourth musical vibe while Van Peebles' off-key gruff singing ("This here's the home of the sheriff, not the land of the free/In America, folks don't run through the streets blood streamin' out from where they've been beaten/In the park for the people and the cop in the good ol' USA, don't think they some kinda gods either") throws darts at freedom, justice and the AmeriKKKan way. In 2011, Van Peebles was shocked when the song was used by the Occupy Wall Street movement in a number of their videos.

Released on Beverly Hills Records, which was also the home of Ozzie Nelson and Jaye P. Morgan, the *Watermelon Man* album contained eleven tracks that included the sorrowful acoustic guitar strumming of "Where Are the Children," a track "sung" (more like talked) by the film's co-star Estelle Parsons. Though it starts simply, it soon develops into a Bacharach-type song with strings and flugelhorn, while Parsons does her weepy white woman rap.

Although his soundtrack work can't compare with the best of Curtis Mayfield (*Super Fly*), Isaac Hayes (*Shaft*) or Marvin Gaye (*Trouble Man*), those dudes cared about being on the charts whereas Van Peebles was simply crafting unconventional compositions. *Watermelon Man* is either completely brilliant, totally bullshit or, as I believe, a weird combination of the two.

Godfrey Cambridge: A Look Back

Godfrey Cambridge possessed a remarkable talent that stretched well beyond his work in *Watermelon Man*. Unfortunately, he and his artistic contributions have been largely overlooked as time has passed.

He was born Godfrey MacArthur Cambridge on February 6, 1933, to parents Sarah and Alexander Cambridge, who were immigrants from British Guyana and Sydney, Nova Scotia. Before coming to the United States, Sarah had been a stenographer and a teacher. In New York City, however, she was relegated to working in the garment district. Alexander had previously been a bookkeeper, but in America he worked a number of blue collar jobs.

Distrusting of, and dissatisfied with, the New York public school system, Cambridge's parents sent him to live with his grandparents in Sydney, Nova Scotia, where they believed he would receive a better education. Later, at the age of thirteen, Cambridge returned to New York City where he attended Flushing High School in Queens. In 1949, he received a four-year scholarship to study medicine at Hoffstra College. In his third year of college, Cambridge left school to pursue his dreams of becoming an actor.

He claimed to have fully come to grips with being black and the added pressures and obstacles that came with that when he entered adulthood. "All my life I ignored being colored," he said. "I never felt racial prejudice because I was the only negro. It's terrible for someone to reach the age of twenty-one and realize he's a negro."

While searching for acting gigs, he worked a variety of day jobs, including cabbie, ambulance driver, and clerk for the New York Housing Authority. He made his "professional" acting debut in an off-Broadway production of *Take a Giant Step*. He then made his Broadway debut in an original production of Herman Wouk's *Nature's Way*. In 1962, he appeared in a role writer/director/actor

Ossie Davis had written specifically with him in mind for, in *Purlie Victorious*. Cambridge would receive a Tony Award nomination for his work in the film, which also featured Davis, Ruby Dee, and Alan Alda, among others. He also co-founded the Committee for the Employment of Negro Performers that same year with Hugh Hurd and Charles Gordon.

Cambridge married actress and producer Barbara Ann Teer in 1962. They would have two daughters before divorcing in 1965.

Cambridge's screen work began with uncredited appearances on the television series *The Phil Silvers Show* and *The Defenders*, as well as in the films *The Last Angry Man* and *Splendor in the Grass*. He landed his first credited roles playing three different characters on the television series *Naked City*.

His first credited film role was in the 1963 adaptation of *Purlie Victorious*, *Gone Are the Days!*, in which he reprised the role of Gitlow Judson. In his search for proper film roles, Cambridge found that there were very few roles of substance written for black actors. However, he was not discouraged. He asked producers to give him the opportunity to audition for non-black roles, telling them he could play anything. As a result, Cambridge played an Irishman in *The Troublemaker*, a concert violinist in *The Biggest Bundle*, and a Jewish taxi cab driver in *Bye Bye Braverman*. In this same vein, he had previously played the role of an aged white woman on Broadway in the play *The Blacks*. (This Obie Award-winning performance would foreshadows his work in *Watermelon Man*.)

In 1963, Cambridge helped establishe the improvisational group The Living Premise. Over the course of his career, he would frequently perform as a standup in comedy clubs. His comedy nabbed him three appearances on *The Tonight Show* in 1964. He also recorded four successful comedy albums for Epic Records. These were *Here's Godfrey Cambridge*, *Ready or Not*, *Them Cotton Pickin' Days Is Over*, *Godfrey Cambridge Toys with the World*, and *The Godfrey Cambridge Show: Recorded Live at the Aladdin, Las Vegas*. One of Cambridge's jokes was that white audiences couldn't tell black actors apart, so he was constantly mistaken for Sidney Poitier. (On a side note, Poitier's nickname for Cambridge was "God".) Cambridge also joked that "people are now referring to Cary Grant as the white Godfrey Cambridge."

One of the reasons for Cambridge's universal appeal during a time of great racial turmoil may have been his reluctance in performing predominantly race-based comedy material. "If I would do just racial material, I'd go out of my cotton-picking mind," he said. "If something happens to me and it's in a black context, then fine. But I don't feel I have to use my race." He did, however, have some comedy routines about race. For instance, one of his most famous bits was about black people putting watermelons inside bowling bags on the way home from the grocery store and passing them off as bowling balls to keep from being embarrassed.

In 1965, Cambridge won an Emmy Award for his appearance on the premiere episode of the experimental comedy series, *Stage II.* In 1967, *Ebony* magazine estimated that Cambridge was making a quarter of a million dollars a year. He continued to find steady work on television and received a ten-year contract with ABC-TV in 1968. That same year, he was nominated for Male New Face by the Laurel Awards. Cambridge, who occasionally wrote for *Monocle* magazine, also managed to publish a book somewhere in there titled *Put Downs and Put Ons*. Not only that, Cambridge also created a board game called "Fifty Easy Steps to the White House."

As Cambridge found success, he used his platform for social activism. One instance of this was his publicly criticizing cabbies who refused to carry black passengers. He wrote about the subject at length, performed a famous comedic routine he called "How to Hail a Taxi," and most importantly, he filed and won a suit against a Manhattan cab company. Another instance was a show he co-produced and directed with his friend Maya Angelou called *Cabaret for Freedom*. The show, which featured songs and dance, comedy routines, and skits was created to help raise money for Martin Luther King Jr.

After appearing in a string of films including *The President's Analyst*, *The Busy Body*, and the aforementioned films, Cambridge was cast in the memorable role of Gravedigger Jones in Ossie Davis' Chester Himes adaptation *Cotton Comes to Harlem*. It is important to note that the film was just the second Hollywood production helmed by an African-American filmmaker (Gordon Parks' *The Learning Tree* was the first). Following *Cotton*, Cambridge would next play the lead in the third Hollywood production in history to have an African-American director.

That film was, of course, Melvin Van Peebles' *Watermelon Man*. During production, Cambridge told *Jet* magazine, "This picture will appeal particularly to those persons who find no difference in a man's race, creed or color. That is, of course, unless they is color blind." At the time he was cast, however, the film was titled *The Night the Sun Came Out on Happy Hollow Lane*. Cambridge and Van Peebles reportedly butted heads throughout filming. When Van Peebles changed the title of the film to *Watermelon Man* (after the 1962 Herbie Hancock song of the same name), Cambridge took offense because he felt that the title was "degrading and offensive." He believed it was an "insulting title" that mocked blacks and trivialized their struggles. This had always been important to the actor/comedian, who sought to portray positive black characters on screen. He said, "I've got a responsibility to those twenty million black folks out there" and also "I'm interested in black kids having heroes. I've given up being ashamed of Africa, ashamed of who I was, ashamed of that hair pomade because I didn't have any heroes." As a result of his disdain for the film's title, Cambridge refused to promote the film. Van Peebles and Cambridge exchanged words in the press. Finally, Cambridge finished the argument with this ludicrous statement in *Jet* magazine: "If this character continues his ranting I'm going to challenge him to a duel—in a watermelon patch!"

Cambridge next appeared in a 1971 episode of *Night Gallery* titled "Make Me Laugh"/"Clean Kills and Other Trophies." The episode was written by series creator Rod Serling and is significant because Cambridge's segment was directed by a young Steven Spielberg.

Throughout his career, Cambridge struggled with his weight. He joked about this, saying that he was eating as a form of racial activism. "Right now, it's not a question of getting served at the counter. It's a matter of eating too much. I never got served before, but now I have to eat at all the restaurants. The food is so good and I'm eating so well that I can't sing 'We Shall Overcome,' I have to burp it." He also joked about occasionally taking trips to health food restaurants. "I go there when I have an attack of wanting to feel healthy. Also, I like to look at people who eat in health food stores because they look so awful. They always look like the underside of a whale." Cambridge went on a variety of fad diets in an effort to lose weight, including Alvenia Fulton's diet, which was trendy among black celebs of the time including Dick Gregory, Eartha Kitt, Roberta Flack, Mahalia Jackson, and Redd Foxx. Because of his constant dieting coupled with his inability to curb his eating habits, Cambridge's weight fluctuated wildly. At one point, he went from three-hundred-and-ten pounds to two hundred and three, later regaining most of it.

Cambridge was originally slated to star in the television series *The Partners*, but quit while filming the pilot due to difficulties with actor/creator Don Adams. Of the dispute, he would later say, "On the set, Don Adams turns into Captain Queeg. He doesn't have those steel balls, but he drove me crazy. Now he's saying, 'The chemistry wasn't right.' Don is so uptight. Finally you have to say to him, 'Hey, man, the price ain't right. I'm willing to get off. I still have the original lining of my stomach. You can't buy a stomach for $25,000. I'll get out while I still have my own.' If you tried to find out who in this industry hates Don Adams the most, the line would run all the way to Phoenix."

In 1972, Cambridge reprised his role as Gravedigger Jones in the *Cotton Comes to Harlem* sequel, *Come Back Charleston Blue*. Although Cambridge's co-star, Raymond St. Jaques, also returned, Ossie Davis did not.

Cambridge spent most of the 1970s semi-retired, occasionally appearing in a film or television show. In 1973, he starred in Oscar Williams' *Five on the Black Hand Side*.

In 1974, the civic-minded Cambridge financed and starred in a twenty-five-minute anti-drug educational film titled *Dead Is Dead*. "Most of us are addicts, living in an addicted society," Cambridge declared. "From the cradle to the grave, we are taught not to deal with stress, problems, anxiety, troubles, or worries. Instead, we are told by the media to get fast, fast relief. Take a pill. If you're feeling really depressed, get relief, take a pill. Take it whether it's for colds, backaches, or anything. Take something and it will go away. It usually doesn't, but it does cause a lasting habit pattern, so it's easy for us to become victims of drug pushers. Because when it comes to drugs, pill pushers and pill takers, we are a country virtually out of control."

The following year, Cambridge married his second wife, Audriano Meyers, whom he would remain married to until his death. They would have two children together. That same year, he appeared alongside Pam Grier and Yaphet Kotto in Arthur Marks' *Friday Foster*. Although Cambridge received third billing, he only appears in the film for a mere four minutes. Although he hadn't planned it, *Friday Foster* would be Cambridge's final theatrical appearance.

On November 29, 1976, Cambridge would suffer a fatal heart attack on the Warner Bros. set for the telefilm *Victory at Entebbe*, in which he was portraying Ugandan president Idi Amin. It is widely accepted that the actor's life-long struggle with his weight played a role in his death. Godfrey Cambridge was forty-three-years-old. His funeral was held on December 1, 1976 at the Hollywood Church of the Hills. He was then interred in Forest Lawn Cemetery. His funeral was attended by cavalcade of black entertainers, including Sidney Poitier, Diahann Carroll, William Marshall, Nancy Wilson, Cicely Tyson, and Raymond St. Jacques.

After Cambridge's death, actor Moses Gunn paid homage to the actor while portraying Martin Luther King Jr. in the Broadway play *I Have a Dream*. At curtain call, Gunn solemnly said, "Wherever you are, Godfrey, I hope you're still giving taxi drivers hell!"

As for Cambridge's legacy, Trav SD sums it on his *Travalanche* blog: "There's no way in hell Cambridge didn't help to drastically rewire the white American public's impressions of black America, let alone of African-Americans in show business. The distance between Stepin Fetchit and Godfrey Cambridge is not just far, it's dimensional. Both were actors, comedians, and artists. But they seem to be operating in entirely different planes of existence. Racists could insist upon hating Godfrey Cambridge if that was their unnatural bent, but they'd have to do some hardcore lying to themselves to pretend a guy like that was inferior. It was becoming possible for African-Americans of precocious intellect to be themselves in mass media without downplaying or apologizing for their gifts. At the same historical moment Cambridge was gaining a foothold in show business, CBS pulled *Amos 'n' Andy* off the air due to pressure from the NAACP. The metamorphosis was that rapid."

TALKING WITH PRODUCTION ASSISTANT CASSIUS WEATHERSBY

Cassius Weathersby claims to be the first black crew member working in Hollywood. He is one of the many unsung heroes in the history of black Hollywood. In the 1960s and early '70s, there were very, very few black people working in Hollywood. This is why Melvin Van Peebles being the *third* black Hollywood director remains significant; although he was preceded by Gordon Parks Jr. and Ossie Davis, it was still a monumental achievement. In this same way, guys like Cassius Weathersby and his friend, the late stunt coordinator Eddie Davis' behind-the-scenes contributions were also significant. Their work (and the work of others who followed) was deemed so trivial by Hollywood that much of it went uncredited. However, Weathersby and these others laid the groundwork for black Hollywood as we know it today.

As I learned quickly (and you will too), Weathersby was not a fan of Van Peebles. Although he never comes out and actually says what Van Peebles did to him on the set of *Watermelon Man*, it seems easy enough to figure out (at least partially) from what he does say. (I'm leaving that up to you, the reader, to decide for yourself.)

Perhaps the most interesting aspect of this interview is Weathersby's repeated assertion that Van Peebles did not want the minority crew members that were hired to work on *Watermelon Man* there. The reason this is interesting is because Van Peebles himself is the man who is generally credited with insisting they be hired. So, what is the truth? This was fifty years ago, so people's memories of events from that time can be clouded. However, Weathersby's repeated assertion (which sounded completely casual and very much had the ring of truthfulness) that Van Peebles did not want the minority crew members on the picture and treated them unkindly brings what we thought we knew previously into question. And if one believes Weathersby (and why wouldn't we?), then that brings forth another question: If Van Peebles didn't make the decision to hire those six individuals, then who did? Was it Columbia Pictures simply seeking positive press and pinning the credit onto the director?

At this late date, we'll likely never know the truth. Perhaps there is some nuance or additional behind-the-scenes information we aren't aware of. And while Weathersby's isn't a particularly glowing remembrance of working with the late director, and while the assertion that Van Peebles didn't want the minority crew members working on his film would seem at odds with the objective of this book—a volume intended to celebrate Van Peebles and his Hollywood film debut—it is important because it possibly sheds some light on aspects of Van Peebles we weren't aware of before. Neither Weathersby's claims nor my questioning Van Peebles' possible motives are intended to cast aspersions. Human beings are complex, and as such, no person is just one thing; each of us is comprised of things that are both positive and negative. Van Peebles was a human being and was no different. In order for us to try to understand who Van Peebles the artist truly was, and how he created the art he created, it is important to look objectively at all of the available information. We weren't there, so none of us (beyond Van Peebles, Weathersby, and a few others) can definitively say what happened.

If what Weathersby says is true and Van Peebles didn't want those crew members working on his film, we cannot properly judge or assess him without knowing the full context. Certainly no one has ever questioned (at least publicly that I am aware of) Van Peebles' loyalty to, affinity for, and pride in the black community. Weathersby suggests here that Van Peebles' motives may have been the result of industry politics.

ANDREW J. RAUSCH: *You worked as a production assistant on* Watermelon Man. *There were six minority crew members hired to shadow the existing crew members. Were you one of those six?*

CASSIUS WEATHERSBY: Yes. I had already been working. I was the very first black person in Hollywood to get a job behind the scenes. I wasn't interested in acting or anything like that. I was a behind the scenes person. That's what I was basically trying to do. I've done a lot of films. I've done about eighty movies in different capacities. But I started out with Melvin Van Peebles, who was not a very nice person. I just didn't think he was that nice of a person.

AR: *He had a reputation for being pretty arrogant at that time. Do you think that's accurate?*

CW: Yes, it is. It sounds right, because he was... He kind of chewed me out a lot because I was asking questions and trying to learn as much as I could. He didn't like that. I don't think he liked me being on the set. [Laughs.] But I was just trying to learn what I could. I was one of the six people that they selected in various capacities. Eddie Smith [a famed stuntman] and I were kind of ringleaders in that respect.

AR: *Since Melvin Van Peebles was only the third black director to work in Hollywood, obviously, he was going to have a place in history. But would you, at the time, have thought that he would become the legend he's now become?*

CW: I don't believe he's a legend, as far as I'm concerned. I'm not trying to talk against him. He had just done a little film [*The Story of a Three-Day Pass*], and he just didn't... We didn't warm up to each other because he knew I was the kind of person who was looking to get work on other projects. And he was reluctant, I guess, to give us work since. When I asked a question, he wouldn't give me a straight answer. His answer didn't matter to me. He didn't answer the questions I had put to him correctly. He was just bothered by the fact that we got six people to work on the project.

AR: *Melvin was an inspiration to a lot of people, but I believe he exaggerated stories about his films to build up his image. I don't mean that as a bad thing, because real or not, the image he created still inspired people. Do you think that's correct?*

CW: Yes, I do, because there weren't many black folks getting jobs, or minorities getting jobs at the time. And I was the one who was pushing hard, *myself*, to get people jobs. Including myself, I also got my sister a job as a wardrobe person because she was into wardrobe. Just minorities who were able to get work on a feature film in Hollywood, even though it was Melvin Van Peebles. And I'm sure he didn't like that very much. I didn't particularly care for him much, because he chewed me out the very first minute. I don't wanna say what happened, but I kind of went against him in certain things. And he didn't like that, you know. I wasn't doing it from a perspective that he is the director and all that; I was coming from the fact that other people were looking for jobs, and I didn't want him to stop us from getting work. He's passed away now, and I don't wanna say anything to demean him, but I didn't particularly care for him.

AR: *What do you remember about Godfrey Cambridge on that project?*

CW: I loved Godfrey! Godfrey and I got along good. I was enjoying the fact that he was on the film, because there were very few black people on it. He was a person I could talk to and related to, even though I was just there to work and try to help other people get jobs. That was my whole thing, trying to get jobs for minorities. It was most black folks at the time trying to get work.

I don't think Melvin really wanted us on the film, to be honest with you. I don't think he wanted us on the film because [he was worried] we would mess up his thing.

AR: *I've been told that Godfrey Cambridge and Melvin didn't get along very well. And they do seem like completely different kinds of people. Do you remember them clashing?*

CW: No, I don't remember that. I just remember the way I was pissed at Melvin. Melvin did an awful thing to me, but I don't even want to go into that. But I was a person who spoke up. I wasn't holding back anything. I was just a person that liked to speak up. And I guess he didn't like what I was saying. I was only trying to get other people jobs, and he was probably against that. He didn't want me to spoil his thing. I understand certain aspects of what he was trying to accomplish, but I was only trying to help other minorities get on the project.

AR: *What did you think of the finished film?*

CW: *Watermelon Man*? I liked it. I thought it was a pretty decent film.

I just didn't like the way Melvin approached people or spoke to people. He wasn't that nice a person. I had it out with him, I really did. I'm not gonna go into it... He did something to me, and then I did something... [Laughs.] Some things happened between him and I, because I was trying to push for other people to get jobs on the film, and he didn't want that at all. He was not really interested in getting jobs for minorities. He was just interested in protecting himself. As far as I know, he'd only done that *Three-Day Pass* thing at the time.

I don't want to say something I'm not supposed to say, but I will tell you that Van Peebles and I did not get along at all.

AR: *You've done a lot in Hollywood, and like you said, you were one of the first black people to work on a film crew. How did you break in?*

CW: I went and found out and asked people... I was the kind of person who wasn't afraid to ask questions and talk to the people who were doing these things. I just interviewed some people that were supposedly important production people. I knew a couple of people who were doing things, like Eddie Smith, who was a stunt coordinator. He was also doing the kind of stuff I was doing. So he and I worked together a little bit. But it was not easy to get into Hollywood. But my sister, she was a wardrobe person. She wanted to do wardrobe, and they let her get in and do certain things. She's no longer with us. Like you said, a lot of them have passed away. I'm getting close to ninety-years-old myself.

AR: *So, do you have any fond memories of working on* Watermelon Man, *or does the stuff with Melvin overshadow everything else?*

CW: Melvin's thing kind of overshadowed it because... I don't wanna go into what he did to me, but he wasn't very nice. But he was afraid of opening the doors the way I wanted to, and I started talking against him in a sense. I said, "We're here to get more minorities work. To get black folks, Latins, people like that jobs." But he wasn't about to do that. He was just trying to get his little movie made. I was coming at it different, and he kind of went off on me. I was trying to bring on the most talented black folks that I knew who were looking for work like myself. I was in there for the long haul, whatever that long haul was. But it didn't really work out for me and him. I don't wanna say what he did to me, but he kind of got into my head a little bit. He was a little violent. It wasn't good at all, and it kind of shocked me when he did it. He wanted to knock some sense into me, and that didn't work. [Laughs.]

AR: *You worked on the movie, and I've verified that fact with other people. But you didn't receive a credit on the movie. Do you think Melvin had something to do with that?*

CW: Of course! He didn't want any of us to get credit. But at the time, those credits, things like PA's, weren't that important. But I started getting involved in film around '61, '62. Eddie Smith and I worked together trying to get jobs for black people as stuntmen, stunt coordinators. I was just there to help people like that, directors who wanted to get into the business as Production Managers or Assistant Directors. I helped out with what I could do.

But Melvin Van Peebles and I did not get along at all. We were not friends at all, even though he was a black person and I was trying to help black people. He was one black person that I would never want to help again. He wasn't a good person at all. He's not somebody that I look up to.

A CONVERSATION WITH ASSISTANT TO THE PRODUCER IVAN C. BECKOFF

Ivan C. Beckoff worked on *Watermelon Man* as the assistant to producer John B. Bennett. (That's a lot of middle initials.) It stands to reason that someone working in such a capacity may not have much information or insight to provide about the picture, but I spoke to him anyway, thinking if nothing else he might be able to provide a few new tiny details here and there. Besides, Beckoff is (at the time of this writing) one of the last survivors who worked on the film. (By my count, there are less than ten people who worked on *Watermelon Man* that are still alive.)

IVAN C. BECKOFF: I was a twenty-three-year-old schnook, right out of film school when I got this job. And here I am turning seventy-seven next week. That's a lot of water under the bridge!"

ANDREW J. RAUSCH: *Are you surprised to be doing an interview about* Watermelon Man *fifty years later?*

IB: Surprised is an understatement.

AR: *What kind of movie did you think you were making at the time?*

IB: I didn't give a shit. I was so happy to have a job at Columbia Pictures. It was just amazing. I mean, just down the hall was [John] Frankenheimer's office, and upstairs was William Wyler's office.

AR: *What was it like working with John Bennett?*

IB: Well, let me preface this by saying that if you want me to talk about Melvin, I can't. The whole time I was there I exchanged *maybe* ten words with Melvin. For a couple of reasons. One, I was white, and two, I was the lowest man on the totem pole. So why should he even give me the time of day? Melvin's son, Mario, was around the set quite a bit. He was just a kid, maybe eight-years-old, hanging out.

I did chat with Godfrey Cambridge a bit. He struck me as a very sweet guy. And I had very good converation with Estelle [Parsons], but I can't remember what we talked about. I probably wanted to know about *Bonnie and Clyde.*

AR: *Were you on the set much?*

IB: A little bit. I'd go down every once in a while to watch shooting. It was not a very big deal picture for Columbia, that's for sure. The original title was *The Night the Sun Came Out on Happy Hollow Lane*. Nobody liked that, and they wanted to do *Watermelon Man* but they thought they had too many racist connotations, until Melvin came on to the picture and gave it the okay.

I even met Herman Raucher. He came out. He was a New York-based writer. He came out for a couple of days, and I met him. But I don't remember much. I mean, we're talking about fifty-odd years ago.

AR: *I was told that Godfrey Cambridge and Melvin Van Peebles didn't get along on the set. Since you were working with the producer, I wondered if you caught wind of any of that?*

IB: I can't comment on that. I think Melvin had very little to do with John Bennett after he was hired. And since he was getting the picture underway, John was more interested in getting another deal for another picture done than he was with this picture. John Bennett was not a real creator/producer on this thing.

AR: *I get that you didn't know Melvin Van Peebles, but what was your perception of him when you saw him around?*

IB: He had a certain degree of, I would say, arrogance. That's the word I would use. But maybe that was a thing he needed since he was the only black man in that position. Except for Gordon Parks maybe. And going back to Oscar Micheaux. There weren't a whole lot of black directors. Or even black actors. Sidney Poitier was there, but there weren't a whole lot of black people working in Hollywood in those days.

AR: *What do you remember specifically about your job? What were some things you did in that position?*

IB: I got the job because I had a friend named Robert who was working at Columbia. And Robert got the job because he was married to a woman named Kate Foreman. Do you know who Carl Foreman is?

AR: *He was the screenwriter on* Bridge on the River Kwai.

IB: Yes. It was his daughter, so he was tight with the executives at Columbia, and they gave his daughter's husband a job. I was a friend of his in film school. Then he told me about John Bennett needing an assistant, so I went up and I got the job.

AR: *What kind of stuff did John Bennett have you doing?*

IB: John Bennett had been an agent, and all of his buddies were agents. He was a producer at Columbia Pictures, so all of his buddies were submitting screenplays to him for possible production. And I was the guy who read these screenplays and wrote synopses of them. I was a D-Girl before there were D-Girls. So I wrote the synopsis. And John was also kind of the low man on the producers totem pole. He wasn't getting A-level material, let me tell you. So I read them, I wrote synopses, and then we'd talk about them. I think there was one he tried to pursue.

What else? ... We used to get weekly budget reports saying where all the money was spent. I used to go over them to see how the budget was tracking. And even in those days, boy, they charged you for every nail.

That's basically what I did. I just hung around. I was kind of in awe just being there.

AR: *Did you get a feel at all for what the studio thought of the picture while it was in production?*

IB: It was a low-budget picture. I don't know, maybe they were trying to be [progressive]. They knew it wasn't going to be a Blaxploitation film, for God's sake. They knew they could do it cheap. I'm trying to remember what the budget was. It might have been as low as seventy-five thousand dollars in 1970 dollars. Which would be about three million dollars today, which is still a pretty cheap film. In those days, the average studio picture cost about three million dollars. I know that Godfrey got fifty-thousand dollars. I think Estelle was making about the same, but I'm not sure. I think John's fee was also fifty-thousand dollars. And I was getting seventy-five dollars a week. I was living on three hundred dollars a month at that time, and I thought I was living on high cotton.

AR: *Do you have any memories of the production that stand out for you?*

IB: I remember there's a scene with Gunnilla Knutson [editor's note: he is mistaken here and is actually referring to a different Swedish model/actress, "Kay Kimberly"]. They called her the "Take It Off Girl" because she did a series of commercials for Noxema. There was a nude scene, and that attracted a lot of attention. All the executives came down to the set that day.

You know, watching a picture being made is like watching paint dry. It's not very exciting. These old union guys were sitting around on the set, and they would rather talk about their golf game. They were not interested in cinema, that's for damn sure. It was just a job for these guys.

AR: *Did you see* Watermelon Man *in the theater when it was released?*

IB: Yes, I did.

Let me tell you one thing I did do. I shot a film. I borrowed some lights and a camera from the USC film department. It's a really big deal now, but in those days… I was told that, as years went by, the building that the cinema department was in was used as a stable for horses. Anyhow, I grabbed a camera and some lights and I shot the application of the makeup on Godfrey. I don't know what ever happened to the film. They were hoping to get it on *The Tonight Show* or something. But I don't think anything ever came of it.

Today, I don't believe that makeup would pass muster. But no one had done it before, so what could you do? Just spread this goop over him and, you know.

AR: *I think it's interesting that we've seen this done since, where guys like Eddie Murphy and Dave Chappelle have played white characters.*

IB: I hope Eddie and Dave had a better makeup artist!

AR: *The one thing I can say about the movie is that Godfrey is very animated. It's hard to imagine a different actor pulling that off as well.*

IB: He was a great comedian. He could have had a great career if he hadn't dropped dead. I was very sad when I heard he'd died, because I liked him very much. He gave me a book, *The Art of the Film* [by Ernest Lindgren], and he autographed it at the end of the production.

He was in *The President's Analyst* and… Have you ever seen *Bye Bye Braverman*? I love that film! I swear, they lived by my grandmother's house, honest to God. It's about Jewish people, and I'm a Jewish guy. I didn't grow up in Brooklyn. I grew up when I was six, but I went back often and visited my relatives there. Anyhow, I love that film. Godfrey has a small part as a Jewish taxi cab driver.

AR: *What was your reaction to the final film?*

IB: Well, in those days I was a great lover of the French New Wave, and I'll tell you the truth—I didn't think too much of *Watermelon Man*. But here's an interesting thing... My wife was from Manchester, England. And she said the film was pretty well known in England. That's what she told me. I don't know.

AR: *Imdb doesn't list you as working on any films after* Watermelon Man.

IB: No. That was pretty much the end of my Hollywood career. I did some work as a cameraman and film editor on some documentaries and commercials. That kind of thing. And then I left Los Angeles, which I never liked. So, I just got out of the film business.

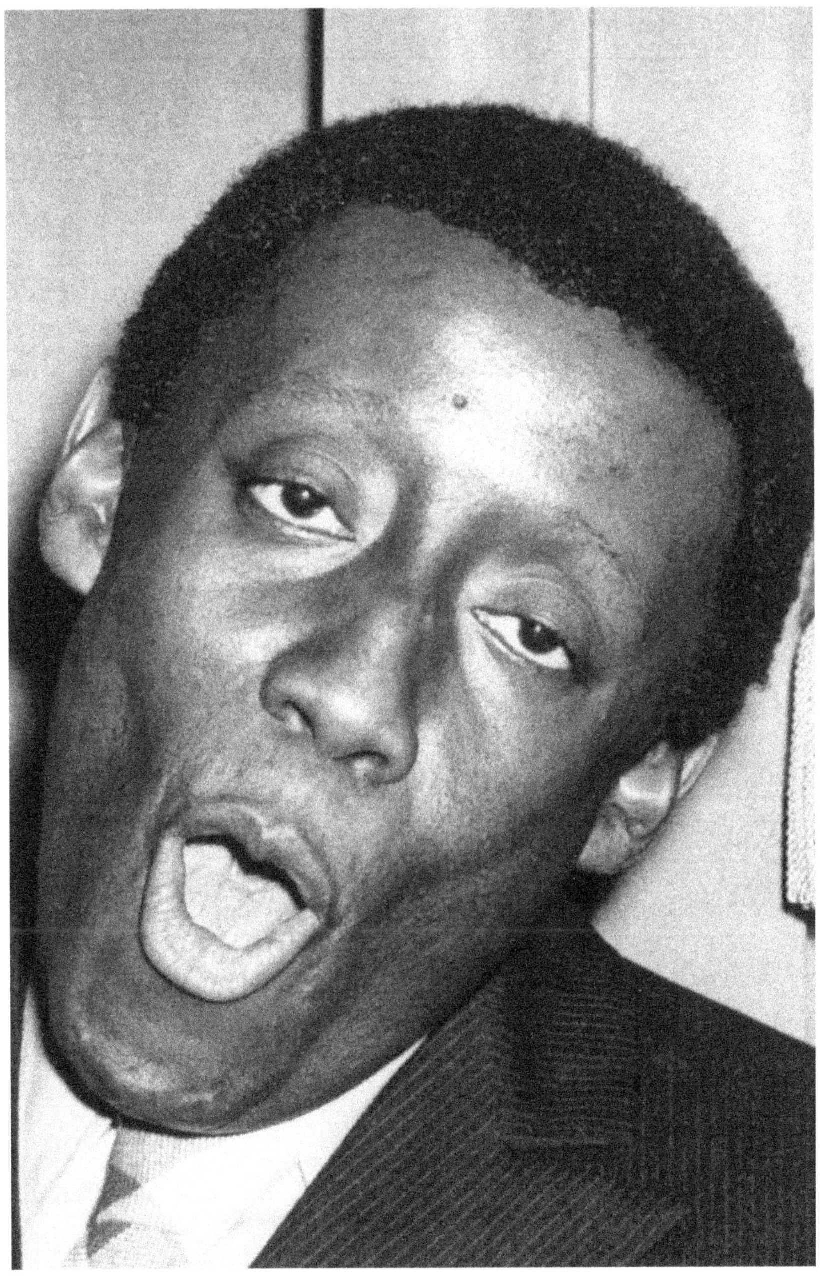

Godfrey Cambridge was known for his fun and affable personality. Here's a photograph of the actor clowning around. (From author's collection.)

The still-white Jeff Gerber sits down to talk with his family. (Columbia Pictures.)

Jeff Gerber thinks he has a tough life, but he will soon find out that life can be much, much more difficult. (Columbia Pictures.)

Known primarily for his bulgy-eyed expression of shock, actor Mantan Moreland had an impressive career spanning more than 130 feature films. (From author's collection.)

Writer and director Melvin Van Peebles looking dapper. (From author's collection.)

By the end of the film, Jeff Gerber has experienced enough of the struggles of being a black man that he picks up a weapon and trains to fight. (Columbia Pictures.)

Watermelon Man *was conceived by novelist and screenwriter Herman Raucher. However, Raucher disliked Van Peebles' finished film. (From author's collection.)*

Oscar-winning actress Estelle Parsons plays Jeff Gerber's fair-weather wife, Althea. (From author's collection.)

Erin Moran, who appears in the film as Jeff's daughter, Janice, would later become famous playing Joanie on the TV show Happy Days. (From author's collection.)

Melvin Van Peebles (From author's collection.)

Godfrey Cambridge (Columbia Pictures)

IDENTITY CRISIS AND SWEETBACK'S BELLYFUL OF A THREE-DAY WATERMELON MAN

by Garrett Chaffin-Quiray

As a novelist, memoirist, playwright, musician, composer, actor, editor, director, producer, options trader and icon of black American cinema, Melvin Van Peebles is a difficult man to pin down. Still active today, he's most closely associated with Sweet *Sweetback's Baadasssss Song*, although this association tends to eclipse his other works and contributions.

Yet Van Peebles is indeed a notable filmmaker, having established himself in the early 1970s. Over the ensuing decades, largely limited to non-cinematic projects, or else marginalized for his maverick sensibility, he has also been a certifiable juggernaut of creative expression in several media and across several industries.

What follows is a career summary meant to encourage a cinephile's interest precisely because Van Peebles and his art are frequently memorable, over and above the catchphrase, "Watch Out. A baadasssss nigger is coming back to collect some dues." Honored with the French Legion of Honor in 2001, the 2000 Acapulco Black Film Festival's Best International Film Award for *Le Conte du ventre plein* (aka *Bellyful*), the 1999 Chicago Underground Film Festival's Lifetime Achievement Award, the 1987 Children's Live-Action Humanitas Prize for *The Day They Came to Arrest the Book*, a 1972 Tony Award nomination for "Don't Play Us Cheap," two 1971 Tony Award nominations for "Ain't Supposed to Die a Natural Death," along with a Grammy Award nomination and Drama Desk Award for this earlier musical, Melvin Van Peebles is more than a one-note film director.

Born Melvin Peebles on August 21, 1932, in Chicago, Illinois, he grew up during World War II and attended Township High School in Phoenix, Illinois, where he graduated in 1949. After a transitional year at West Virginia State College, he then transferred to Ohio Wesleyan University and earned a Bachelor of Arts degree in English Literature in 1953.

Enlisting in the US Air Force, he met his future wife, Maria Marx, a white woman, in 1955. The two were married and after three and a half years he left the military for Mexico. While there he dabbled as a painter, became a father and eventually moved to San Francisco where he worked as a cable car operator.

Stricken with varied creative interests, he produced a few short films, including *Three Pickup Men for Herrick* and *Sunlight*. He also wrote the text to a children's book called *The Big Heart* and pitched himself to Hollywood talent agents but failed to make a connection. Frustrated by his prospects, he was fired from his job, after which he capitalized on the GI Bill and moved his family—then consisting of wife Maria, son Mario and daughter Megan—to Holland in 1959. He enrolled at the University of Amsterdam to study astronomy, added the qualifier "Van" to his name and continued pursuing creative projects in terms now called "workaholic."

Perhaps due to his ambitions, absenteeism or rumors of infidelity, the couple divorced. Maria returned to the States with Mario and Megan, and Melvin joined the Dutch National Theater where he began acting earnest. To make ends meet he worked as a street performer and sometimes depended on lady friends for a place to live.

Eventually Henry Langlois, founder of the Cinematheque Francaise, saw Van Peebles' short films and invited him to Paris where he spent the next several years singing, dancing, acting and writing the novels *A Bear for the FBI*, *The Chinamen of the 14th District*, *The Party of Harlem* and *La Permission*. Among odd jobs, he edited comic sequences in the French edition of *Mad* magazine and produced the Francophone short *Cing cent balles*.

Learning he could adapt one of his novels into film with a sixty-thousand-dollar grant from the French Cinema Center, so long as his film was "artistically valuable, but not necessarily commercially viable," he sought a producer. Once partnered with the Office de Production d' Edition et de Realisation (OPERA), a collective consisting of Michel Zemer, Guy Pefond and Christian Shivat, he shot *La Permission* in thirty-six days for a cost of $200,000, finally releasing the picture under the title *The Story of a Three-Day Pass*.

It tells the story of Turner (Harry Baird), a black army man who meets a white Parisian named Miriam (Nicole Berger). The pair spends a weekend together, enjoying their romance but also struggling with the complexities of racism. Eventually their miscegenation is reported to Turner's captain (Hal Brav) and he's restricted to barracks where he realizes the futility of such amorous adventures.

The Story of a Three-Day Pass departs from generic convention by focusing on a black hero and embracing New Wave-inspired realist techniques alongside fantasy sequences. Using jump cuts, freeze frames, photomontage and the conceit interracial predation, *The Story of a Three-Day Pass* contains the seeds of Van Peebles' later pursuits. Beyond these experimental techniques, though, the writer-director created a relatively polished and enjoyable love story. Entered as a French film in the 1967 San Francisco Festival organized by black film critic Albert Johnson, *The Story of a Three-Day Pass* allowed Van Peebles to work his way into the Hollywood fold. Contracted with Columbia Pictures he was given a farce. Based on a Herman Raucher script and produced under the working title *The Night the Sun Came Out on Happy Hollow Lane*, Van Peebles scored and directed the film, finally called *Watermelon Man*. Shot in twenty-two days and released with a budget just under one million dollars, it's the story of a bigoted, white insurance executive named Jeff Gerber (Godfrey Cambridge). One day he wakes up a black man and has a number of misadventures before finally embracing his new identity and transforming into a militant revolutionary.

Released in a moment of growing racial unrest and conflict in the United States, *Watermelon Man* mixes serio-comic elements with topical material. Significantly, Cambridge offers an appealing performance that complicates the usual process of identification for mainstream—read white—viewers since he's a black man made up in white face before "waking up" to become himself, a black man.

When given Hollywood's financial troubles during the late 1960s and early '70s, *Watermelon Man* was a troublesome project. Infighting between Columbia's executives and Van Peebles was commonplace. After such wrangling over an appropriate ending, in which Van Peebles ultimately triumphed, the film was released to a domestic theatrical gross of $1,568,315, ranking it as the fifty-sixth most popular film of 1970, well behind the number one title, *Airport* with a gross of $12,378,259. In this sophomore effort, certain stylistic choices from his debut are repeated, including jump cuts and visual counter-point, along with the introduction of filters for melodramatic impact. Altogether these stylistic choices point in the direction of an alternative, non-Hollywood form while also organizing an extremely entertaining, provocative feature.

Van Peebles used his salary from *Watermelon Man* to fund nineteen days of production on *Sweet Sweetback's Baadasssss Song* in late 1970. Budgeted at $500,000 and, at one point, now famously infused with a fifty-thousand dollar loan from Bill Cosby, Van Peebles wrote, directed, co-produced, scored, edited and starred in his most famous movie.

He hired non-union labor and took on the marketing responsibilities himself. He also released the film through Cinemation, a struggling exploitation distributor, and put his limited marketing budget into radio advertisements targeting black audiences. After an X-rating from the Motion Picture Association of America (MPAA), Van Peebles threatened lawsuits against the MPAA but turned the negative rating into a publicity coup. Using the catchphrase "rated X by an all-white jury," he redesigned the film's advertisements and boosted the film's many ancillary markets.

Released to simultaneous acclaim and disdain in both the black and white communities, *Sweet Sweetback's Baadasssss Song* temporarily took the top box office position from the year's number one grossing film, the $50 million earning *Love Story*. It also went on to gross $4.1 million, along with producing certain symbols and stock characters that would be central to black imagery through the present.

As discussed elsewhere by critics like Donald Bogle, Thomas Cripps and Ed Guerrero, *Sweet Sweetback's Baadasssss Song* appeared at the cusp of Blaxploitation. Ignoring other influential movies like *Shaft*, what Van Peebles' film conveyed was the interest and viability of black cultural products independently produced by, and for, a primarily black audience. In 1971 he'd managed to attune his filmmaker's heartstrings to the pulse of his times. Foremost among his goals was the repudiation of accepted mainstream standards about representing black people.

Lacking narrative polish, the expertise of professional actors and production staff, or the groupthink of a corporate publicity department, *Sweet Sweetback's Baadasssss Song* remains a challenging, difficult film. Its success stems from an insider view of black experience. Its failures likewise stem from centering on a criminal with few redeeming qualities.

Beyond producing a hit movie, Van Peebles' great innovation was recognizing the economic impetus supporting the movie industry. Thusly he targeted an under-realized black audience and reaped a small fortune. That Hollywood paid attention adds to the commonly held belief about how *Sweet Sweetback's Baadasssss Song* was then divided from its political ideals to have its stoic lead, popular music, underworld surroundings and sexual situations exported into Blaxploitation.

However true these correlations may seem, the film didn't entirely manage to turn the film industry on its ear. Though annual grosses demonstrate how it was influential in 1971, its larger legacy is in demonstrating artistic ingenuity from a non-mainstream source.

Perhaps due to this independently minded success, or perhaps due to his theatrical pursuits immediately following *Sweet Sweetback's Baadasssss Song*, Van Peebles didn't direct another original feature for almost eighteen years. Turning to the Great White Way, he produced two Broadway musicals, "Ain't Supposed to Die a Natural Death" and "Don't Play Us Cheap," the latter becoming a virtually unseen fourth feature film adaptation in 1973.

"Ain't Supposed to Die a Natural Death" was a commercial disappointment. By contrast, it was also critically lauded and eventually nominated for seven Tony Awards, including Best Book and Score for Van Peebles, not to overlook his Grammy Award nomination and Drama Desk Award.

"Don't Play Us Cheap," adapted from his novel *The Party in Harlem*, exacerbated the troubled box office record of its predecessor but was similarly celebrated for its fantasy elements. Centered on a pair of the devil's minions crashing a boisterous Harlem house party, the musical opened later in the same season as "Ain't Supposed to Die a Natural Death," meaning both shows were on Broadway in simultaneous runs. As a crowning accomplishment, "Don't Play Us Cheap" was itself nominated for two Tony Awards, including another Best Book nod for Van Peebles.

Thereafter he was associated with a number of theatrical productions ranging from cabarets and one-man shows to ensemble dramas and musicals. One result was the play "Out There By Your Lonesome" in 1973. At the same time he was actively promoting his behind the scenes book *The Making of Sweet Sweetback's Baadasssss Song* while also recording several musical and spoken word albums, among them "What the . . . You Mean I Can't Sing?" and "X-Rated by an All-White Jury." A new novel called *The True American* followed in 1976, after which Van Peebles produced the screenplay for *Just an Old Sweet Song*, a television movie.

Throughout the mid-'70s, trade papers reported his attachment to different feature films, although little came of insubstantial rumor. By 1977, however, his Tinsel Town connections seemed poised for renewal after he'd written the script for *Greased Lightning*, a Richard Pryor vehicle. Part way through production, however, he quit and was replaced by Michael Schultz.

Perpetually at odds over being given secure financing and being allowed the freedom to pursue his craft, Van Peebles' relationship with Hollywood continued to stumble along. Still, he worked as an actor and occasionally wrote teleplays. *The Sophisticated Gents* was one such work in which a group of black professionals meet for a twenty-seven-year school reunion and grapple with the changing virtues and faults of their aging selves even as a murder is committed in their midst.

Two plays later, "Waltz of the Stork" in 1981 and "Champeen" in 1983, a lost bet changed the focus of the artist's activities for much of the 1980s. Given his wide social network, he was assisted into the securities industry where he became the first black American to hold a seat on the American Stock Exchange. Associated as a trader with Timber Hill, Inc., he was successful in his new pursuit trading stock options and managing fortunes on a daily basis.

Returning to his literary foundations, *Bold Money: A New Way to Play the Options Market* was the result of applying the new profession to his much older craft. As an explanation of how to use discretionary funds to invest in more volatile positions than are possible in fixed income products like Treasury Bills and CDs, the book was an application of lessons learned in film financing turned to the high yield potential of stock derivatives. Which is to say Van Peebles wrote about using money within the prescribed system to achieve personal satisfaction.

Throughout the '80s he continued guest starring in films and TV shows, frequently with his son Mario, and it's been this collaborative element that has sustained him through the present. *Identity Crisis*, his fifth feature as director, was a product of father and son working together. Starring Mario as a body-switching gay hairdresser who enters the body of a b-boy, the film fell flat with audience and critics alike, all of whom were aware of a late '80s body-switching cycle of films for which *Identity Crisis* provided an unpleasant exclamation point.

A more positive result of this experience was a memoir he co-wrote with his son. Entitled *No Identity Crisis: A Father and Son's Story of Working Together*, the book saw Melvin reflect on his relatively difficult struggle for success set against Mario's more privileged upbringing as a mixed-race child, Ivy League graduate and one time employee of New York City's mayor, Ed Koch.

As Mario's career took off following his film *New Jack City*, Melvin's career became more and more associated with supporting his son's projects. A novel he'd written called *Panther* became the basis for his eponymous script and Mario's movie in 1995. Though drawn from historical events and based on the lives of members of the Black Panther Party, the result was lambasted by critics and ignored at the box office.

Closing on the age of traditional retirement at the end of the twentieth century, Van Peebles has been persuaded to accept the mantle of cultural icon. With home video technologies ceding market share to feature-rich laser discs and DVDs, and with the rise of the hip-hop generation reared on cultural products like various of Van Peebles' creations, the man has become a living symbol and keynote of his times.

Based on a wide-ranging body of work, Melvin Van Peebles is generally concerned with black empowerment and economical control within the white-dominated American system. But history remembers him almost exclusively as the director of *Sweet Sweetback's Baadasssss Song* and this tendency is both habitual and troubling. It suggests a great man theory with limited context while continuing to make his third film the birthplace for Blaxploitation, thus minimizing re-consideration of its influence or of the cycle considered to be its result.

This tendency is likely related to the controversy surrounding *Sweet Sweetback's Baadassss Song* and the other films released in its wake. The tendency may also have something to do with the backlash against Van Peebles for having the audacity to write, direct, co-produce, score, edit and star in a film that deeply inflamed its viewers but was never followed up with the same measure of influence by any of his subsequent projects.

Regardless, Van Peebles' collected works remain for us to categorize, embrace or reject. As just one illustration of an effort to do just that, the New York Museum of Modern Art (MOMA) sponsored a retrospective of his films in June 1990. Though thirteen years have passed since this institutional benchmark, he continues to perform on-stage, on television and in the movies, while his son has seen his star rise with a career organized in very similar fashion to that of his father.

Now a character type all of his own, he continues to be a cigar-smoking curmudgeon dedicated "to all the Brothers and Sisters who had enough of the man." In short, Van Peebles is a maverick spirit and multi-talented creative force, the likes of whom are not often seen.

ESTELLE PARSONS LOOKS BACK ON WATERMELON MAN

by Rob St. Mary

Estelle Parsons is an acting legend who has won or been nominated for just about every acting award (for both stage and screen) there is. Her best-known film is the iconic 1967 film, *Bonnie and Clyde*, for which she snagged the Academy Award for Best Supporting Actress.

Most notably for the purposes of this book, Parsons played Jeff Gerber's wife, Althea, in *Watermelon Man*. She was nominated for the BAFTA Film Award for Best Supporting Actress for her work in the film. Parsons turned in a memorable performance working opposite Godfrey Cambridge, with whom she shared a great chemistry.

ROBERT ST. MARY: *You've had such a great career. A lot of great stuff. It's an honor to get a few minutes to talk to you. So, thanks so much for taking the time.*

ESTELLE PARSONS: The funny thing is, it seems to get greater the older it gets. So that's good.

RSM: *Well, that's good. You never want to feel that you've peaked as an artist, I guess.*

EP: [Laughs.] No, but I mean the movies! Like *Watermelon Man*, you know. What kind of a stir did it make when it came out? I don't know. I don't think much of one. You probably know more about it than I do. But, you know, some of the movies you make, you think, oh my gosh! Then, years later, someone'll meet you on the bus and say, "Oh my Lord, I love such and such!" And you think, wow! You know, they live on forever. Or a little while anyway. I mean in terms of however long the film lasts. But now you don't even shoot on film anymore, so...

RSM: *You were in* Watermelon Man. *I was wondering how that came to be. How did you get cast in the film?*

EP: Melvin Van Peebles, I guess he'd seen me in *Bonnie and Clyde*. I had done another film, *Rachel Rachel*, the next year for Paul Newman. I was up for an Academy Award for that as well. Melvin had done a movie in France called *The Story of a Three-Day Pass*. So he called my lawyer for me to do *Watermelon Man*. He was the first black guy to be shooting a film on the studios out there. You know, they didn't have any money. And the script was kind of weird because it was Melvin. He marches to his own drummer. So all my advisors said not to do it. Because I had a good career and I could pretty much pick and choose what I wanted to do. So they said, "Don't do it, don't do it, don't do it!" But I had this idea that I should support somebody like that, you know, who was trying to break into what was a white establishment thing. I'm never a big fan of that [kind of segregation]. I'm a big multi-culturalist. I'm a very fervent multi-culturalist. So I thought, well, if Melvin wants me to do the movie, I'll do it. That was him and of course, he's a marvelous artist and I very much like him both as a person and as an artist. I thought, if he wants me to do it, I'm gonna do it. So I did it.

RSM: *You said the script was a little odd. What do you remember about reading it and thinking about your part?*

EP: I don't remember reading it or thinking about my part. I don't often do that. When I read a movie script, if I respond to the character right away, like "Oh, I could do that," then I do it. I think if you don't have that response you'd better not do it. Because in the theatre it's quite different. You wanna read something and say, "What is this? How am I gonna do this? Oh my lord, is it even possible?" You wanna do that in the theatre because you've got four weeks to figure it out and get something right for yourself, you know, but in the movies, from my point of view, you wanna read it and say, "Oh boy, that's something I can do." So that's usually the impression I have, and then I usually don't ever look at the script again until we're shooting. I'm not gonna give words on paper very much attention because, you know, they're only words on paper. They're not literature.

RSM: *What do you remember about working with Godfrey Cambridge on the film?*

EP: Oh, I loved Godfrey! Everybody did. He was wonderful. We lived about five buildings apart in New York, and he was just great to work with. It wasn't an easy film to do. We were under so much pressure because of the suits out there and Melvin being black also. It wasn't an easy film to do. But we had a very wonderful time doing it.

We shot it in a very short time. I don't know how much of that is even in what you read about movies. But we shot it much more quickly than most movies are shot. We were always bouncing in and out of the script. We never knew what we were going to do from day to day.

RSM: *Melvin had said he did it in something like twenty, twenty-one days. Something like that. Like three weeks?*

EP: I think so. Yeah. Four weeks.

RSM: *As for working with Melvin, you talked a little bit about him. But what do you remember about him as a person and working with him on the film?*

EP: Well, he's a terrific person. Of course he's terribly smart. He's totally interested in absolutely everything. I mean, as one can see from his whole life now... I think he went into stockbrokering for a while. He's done all kinds of wonderful stuff. And of course, a great composer and musician as well. So, it was very lovely to work for him. And he was very clearly under an awful lot of pressure. And he handled it with an enormous amount of grace and he managed to do things nobody had done before, and make a really decent film out of it all. I thought he was a terrific guy. I liked him very much.

RSM: *I was going to ask you what your thought was when you saw the film completed and out, and what the reactions were that people said to you about it.*

EP: You know, I don't remember ever seeing it. I was very, very busy at that particular time. And I don't remember... Well, yeah, I know I saw it because I remember there was one scene in which I have curlers on and I'm on the telephone. But I don't remember where I saw it or what I thought. I was just so busy. And I had two kids to bring up by myself. So, once I've got the job done, I don't pay very much attention to my movies. Because what's the point? Unless you just like to look at yourself a lot. [Laughs.] They're done. They're there. They are what they are. What possible meaning could they have to you? Except to sit there and say, "One time I was good at that." And another time you look at it with another frame of mind and you say, "Oh, I wasn't so good at that." So, you know...

I know everybody doesn't feel that way. Greg Peck told me I should go to the rushes because he learned a lot from watching his face and [understanding] what he could do with his face. But I'm just not that kind of an actor. You know, I try to inhabit somebody and then I just go forward. I don't like to do a lot of takes. I just get an idea of what I should be doing, and then I try to go for it. So one take is about as much as I want. If I have to do two, okay. And if I have to do twenty, I can do that too. It isn't that, it's just that I'm not interested in it. I'm inhabiting the person, and the person's gonna do what the person's gonna do. And then it's done, and that's it for me. So, I don't give a lot of conscious thought to "do this with your face," "do things with your mouth," "think about this," "say things differently." I really don't do all that stuff.

RSM: *That, to me, sounds very much like someone who understands what they're doing on the stage. Doing it on stage and being in the moment is much more important than, as you said, the minutiae of what a lot of film actors would do.*

EP: Yeah, I think that's good. You might be right about that. Because it is kind of what you do on the stage. You have to get out there each time and just be there and do it. And I know movies are not like that. That's true.

Watermelon Man and *Cotton Comes to Harlem*: Black Filmmaking in Hollywood

by Novotny Lawrence

When motion pictures emerged as a popular form of entertainment, they reaffirmed and perpetuated commonly held stereotypes about black people that affected them socially, economically, and politically. From early silent films such as Thomas Edison's *A Watermelon Eating Contest* to alleged masterpieces like *Gone with the Wind*, blacks were depicted as loyal toms, bumbling coons, sassy and overbearing mammies, tragic mulattoes, and savage bucks, while in film after film their white counterparts were presented as a range of well-rounded, multidimensional characters.

Importantly, Hollywood's discriminatory practices also extended behind the camera as for years Hollywood did not provide blacks opportunities to direct films. In fact, it was not until 1968 that *Life* magazine photographer-turned-filmmaker Gordon Parks became the first man to helm a Hollywood movie when he directed *The Learning Tree*. Two years later, film executives at Columbia Studios and United Artists granted Melvin Van Peebles and Ossie Davis opportunities to seize the means of production on *Watermelon Man* and *Cotton Comes to Harlem*, respectively. Both directors used their films to challenge Hollywood's skewed representations of black identity, life, and culture, and to pave the way for ensuring generations of black filmmakers.

Van Peebles broke into Hollywood via Europe, where he had moved in part due to the lack of opportunities for blacks in Hollywood. While overseas, he made a number of short films and wrote several novels, including *The Story of a Three-Day Pass*, which he adapted for the screen. *Pass* tells the story of Turner, an African-American GI stationed in France, who while on a short leave from his base strikes up a romance with a white French woman named

Miriam. The couple spends two happy nights together professing their love for one another. But their romantic dream is deferred when a group of white G.I.s from Turner's company spots the couple together and reports the interracial romance to their superior officer. Livid to find that he has been courting a white woman, the officer confines Turner to his quarters. By the time he is able to phone Miriam again, he finds that she is off spending time with another man.

Van Peebles submitted *Pass* to the 1967 San Francisco International Film Festival, which he attended as a French delegate. The film was an instant hit, winning the Critic's Choice Award, and Van Peebles was quickly and incorrectly heralded as the U.S.'s first African-American director. In the aftermath of his success, Columbia Studios began aggressively pursuing him. Though initially hesitant to accept the studio's offer, Van Peebles eventually signed a three-picture deal with Columbia and agreed to direct *Watermelon Man*.

Watermelon Man tells the story of Jeff Gerber (Godfrey Cambridge), a privileged and bigoted white man who epitomizes the so-called American Dream. He is firmly middle class, with a wife, two kids, and a nice home in the suburbs. Gerber's perfect existence is thrown into chaos one morning when he awakens to find that overnight he has transformed into a black man. The remainder of the film chronicles Gerber as he learns what it means to live in a society in which black men endure racial discrimination, are fetishized by white women, and face challenges navigating spaces where the color of their skin invites the specter of violence.

At the time of its release, *Watermelon Man* was a unique racial satire, but Van Peebles' experiences with Columbia executives during the production demonstrate the challenges associated with centering blackness in a Hollywood film. Particularly, the director explained, "Columbia's approach to the film was to sacrifice real social commentary on race in favor of making a 'feel good' movie that would appeal to white audiences. Rather than succumbing to the studio's demands and soften what he envisioned as a biting social satire, Van Peebles craftily negotiated the situation. For instance, Columbia execs initially wanted to cast a high-profile white actor such as Jack Lemmon or Alan Arkin to play the lead role in *Watermelon Man*. Van Peebles subtly pushed back, requesting that a black actor star in the film and asking for a supporting role for black actor Mantan Moreland. Aside from that, he left all other casting decisions to the studio.

In addition, Van Peebles expressed concern over *Watermelon Man*'s original ending, which saw Gerber awaken in the middle of the night to find that his transformation into a black man had been nothing more than a bad dream. Leery of Van Peebles' desire for the character to remain black at film's end, Columbia execs agreed to let him shoot two versions of the ending. When the film was completed, they would later determine which to use based on test audiences' reactions to them.

Although casting a black actor and negotiating with execs to shoot two endings may seem like rather small victories, each had a significant impact on *Watermelon Man*. Had a white actor played Gerber, he would have spent the majority of the film in blackface makeup, hearkening back to the minstrel tradition that for decades informed early Hollywood films and black images in popular culture more broadly. By casting black actor and comedian Godfrey Cambridge in the role, Van Peebles inverted blackface performances as Cambridge appeared in a very unconvincing whiteface for the film's first ten minutes. As Racquel Gates explains, "On this micro level of aesthetics, *Watermelon Man* uses whiteface to reverse the logic of whiteness as norm. By placing an African-American actor in white makeup to portray the "normal" Jeff Gerber, the film throws into question the idea of what 'normal' looks like in the first place."

Further, Van Peebles deceived the studio executives by agreeing but never actually shooting *Watermelon Man*'s original ending. Rather than positioning the black experience as a horrible nightmare, Gerber turns revolutionary and, at film's end, trains with makeshift weapons alongside a group of other black men. The implication is that he and the brothers will rise up against the U.S.'s racist system if need be to make sure that blacks' struggles for civil rights are fully realized. Thus, as Gates summarizes, "Melvin Van Peebles' *Watermelon Man*—the result of creative brilliance and sheer force of will—expresses a black-oriented perspective in spite of industrial factors working to actively suppress any manifestation of radical politics."

Before landing the job as director on *Cotton Comes to Harlem*, Ossie Davis had established himself as an actor, writer, and activist. In particular, he had starred in a number of Broadway plays, including *The Wisteria Trees*, *Remains to be Seen*, *No Time for Sergeants*, and *Purlie Victorious*. Davis also appeared in films such as *The Cardinal* and *The Hill*, and on the TV series *Car 54, Where Are You?* and *The Defenders*.

Despite his impressive resume and a strong desire to break into filmmaking, Davis was not initially selected to direct the highly-anticipated *Cotton Comes to Harlem*. The film was a screen adaptation of Chester Himes' Harlem Detectives series, novels the author had hesitantly written while living in France, where he had moved after his previous works, *Lonely Crusade* and *Cast the First Stone*, performed poorly in the United States. Writing in the tradition of hard-boiled novelists Dashiell Hammett and Raymond Chandler, Himes conceived of fantastic tales about two black detectives working to solve crimes on the tough Harlem streets. French (and subsequently African-American) audiences perceived his outlandish vision of Harlem and its residents as authentic representations of the U.S., making the novels international successes. The series captured the attention of Hollywood producer Samuel Goldwyn Jr., who purchased the screen rights to the detective novels with the intention of adapting them into a motion picture franchise.

Goldwyn Jr.'s purchase of the rights to Himes' Harlem Detectives novels initially concerned avid fans of the books, who were "alarmed that the Hollywood moguls—fearful of raps from black integrationists—would bleach out all their hilarious "local color," make everybody talk General American and remove all the special flavor that gave them their special distinction." Cognizant of such concerns, Goldwyn turned to Davis, who had initially been cast as one of the film's lead detectives, to rewrite white screenwriter Arnold Pearl's draft of *Cotton*'s script. Davis provided such a strong revision that Goldwyn Jr. hired him to direct the film. His vision, style, and penchant for centering blackness are apparent from the onset of the film.

Cotton opens by taking viewers on a tour of Harlem as it follows the Rev. Deke O'Malley's (Calvin Lockhart) limousine to the site of a fundraiser that he is holding as a part of his Back to Africa crusade. Convinced that his campaign is nothing more than an attempt to swindle Harlem residents out of their money, police detectives Coffin Ed Johnson (Raymond St. Jacques) and Grave Digger Jones (Godfrey Cambridge) attend to keep watchful eyes on O'Malley. All is well until armed gunmen interrupt the festivities, stealing the eighty-seven thousand dollars in passages that O'Malley has collected and fleeing in a getaway truck. The remainder of the film chronicles Coffin Ed and Grave Digger as they work to bring the culprits to justice and, more importantly, retrieve the stolen money so that they may return it to their Harlem brothers and sisters.

Although *Cotton* follows a standard detective storyline, Davis delivered a fresh take on the longstanding genre. Most notably, the film features two black detectives working in a predominantly black urban locale. Before Cotton, Hollywood films such as *The Maltese Falcon* and *The Big Sleep* centered on lone white detectives like Sam Spade or Philip Marlowe working to solve crimes in cities seemingly devoid of people of color. In directing a film that centers on two cool, confident, hard-nosed black police detectives who remain loyal to the Harlem community, Davis expanded traditional conceptions of the detective genre.

Further, Davis also took direct aim at the longstanding stereotypes that circumscribed black life, culture, and identity, making whites' perpetuation of such distorted mythologies absurd in the process. Particularly, he satirizes the racist notions that blacks love fried chicken and watermelon during two key moments in *Cotton Comes to Harlem*. First, at the end of the sequence in which Coffin Ed Johnson and Gravedigger Jones pursue the thieves who stole the Back to Africa passages, the police detectives crash their car into a watermelon cart. Second, when a crowd of O'Malley supporters gather outside the jail to protest his arrest, they disperse after Coffin Ed and Gravedigger throw live chickens into the crowd. Clearly, the implications in both scenes are that in even the most serious moments blacks' genetic predispositions for watermelon and fried chicken will soothe their souls. By taking aim at the stereotypes in such key moments, Davis positions them as ridiculous constructions conceived in the white imagination.

We are currently witnessing a groundswell of black films made by black directors. For instance, Ava DuVernay has established herself as one of Hollywood's most notable filmmakers with movies like *Selma* and the Netflix documentary *13th*. Additionally, in 2017 Jordan Peele burst onto the cinematic landscape with his black-themed horror film *Get Out* and further showcased his ability to center blackness in the horror genre with his 2019 follow-up, *Us*.

As we continue to enjoy those directors' films, it is important to remember that they are the descendants of Van Peebles and Davis. Fifty years ago, they worked within the Hollywood studio system to advance representative examinations of blackness and critiques of U.S. racism.

Consequently, *Watermelon Man* and *Cotton Comes to Harlem* remain milestones that helped galvanize black filmmaking in Hollywood and illustrate that on cinema screens representations of black life, culture, and identity matter.

SPITTIN' WATERMELON SEEDS

by Darius James

I hadn't seen *Watermelon Man* for decades. I'd been familiar with Melvin's work since teenhood, so I was no stranger to this film. In fact, I first saw a screening of *Sweet Sweetback's Baadasssss Song* during my post-flag-burning sophomore year in high school, despite its triple XXX rating. Melvin was in attendance. He did a Q&A at Yale's drama school (his opening statement was spectacular, saying *The American Dream is the black man's nightmare in the white man's reality!* Or something to the effect. (Whatever it was, it put "woke" rhetoric to shame.) So, to reacquaint myself, I shelled out some shekels to Jeff Bezos on my debit card and streamed it on Amazon.

I watched. I was *irritated*.

The last time I checked it out, I was a goofy fifteen-year-old. I saw it at a seedy drive-in while blasting weed and guzzling apple wine with some weedhead homies. Godfrey Cambridge was the "hip" black comedian at the time; headlining the Playboy Club and throwing barbs at whitey like Bruce Lee's ninja stars. Yet, white folks loved the shine on his black behind. *Time* magazine said Cambridge was the funniest man in America (well, in 1965, anyway. Dick Gregory was staging a hunger strike in a Mississippi county jail, probably.) He sparkled in *The President's Analyst*; shiving a muthafucka in the garment district, disguised in a doo-rag and gleaming conk. So now, after successfully playing a Negro, it was time to kick open the doors of the storefront church, break out buckets of fried chicken and celebrate. Hollywood had crowned him a *White Man!*

And me with my nickel bag was there to see it...

Originally cast in *Popi* as a Puerto Rican (and paired with the eyeball-popping Rita Moreno), Columbia studios wanted *Wait Until Dark*'s scary-ass dopefiend Alan Arkin in the lead.

Why not smudge him up with some burnt cork?

America had a long history of minstrelsy's cowbell-clangin' Endmen—from lavish plantation shows to Mickey Mouse rolling his keister in *Steamboat Willie* ["I do not understand your Disneyland! You have a black mouse with a white voice!"—Richard Pryor as Idi Amin]. Hell, in 1969, a year before the release of *Watermelon Man*, Robert Downey Sr., decades ahead of his son slapping on blackface in *Tropic Thunder*, voiced the titular character of *Putney Swope* in post-production—an underscored exception to the rule in blackface history—due to Arnold Johnson's inadequate line reading. Blackface was, in fact, not only the country's first dominant form of mass entertainment, serving up silver-plattered white supremacy in music halls from coast to coast, it kicked off the revolution with that whole King's tea party in Boston Harbor thing.

However, when hired-gun Melvin Van Peebles stepped into the ring, he insisted on a black actor to carry the film. This would be far more cost effective. A black actor only had to endure the laborious make-up process for a few whiteface scenes in the first act's opening moments.

Mo' blackface. *Mo'* money.

The studio conceded. During its 1970 release, the film was hyped as a marvel of make-up wizardry; celebrated as a dubious at best Jackie Robinson-like achievement by Hollywood media. "*Wow! He really does look like a son of the Caucasus mountains!!!*" (if, of course, looking like a son of the Caucasus mountains meant the color of your skin matched the color of Silly Putty). Jeff Gerber not only looked like a guy who sold homeowners insurance to Barbie's Malibu Dream House, he looked like the stuff the house was made out of too: *plastic*. He would have looked more at home on the set of *Star Trek: The Next Generation*. Data's bigoted android buddy. Ultimately, Melvin's watermelon joke questions the artificial basis of whiteness's own self-conception.

Watermelon Man opens by panning across a charmless suburban bedroom to patriotic military music conducted by someone with a brain disorder. The camera tilts up, tilts down, to a clumsy off-screen thump. Then it slides along the surface of a bureau, covered with the accoutrements of present-day corporate slavery, and reveals a sauna-suited Jeff Gerber (Godfrey Cambridge) skipping rope. *Thud. Thud. Thud.* Pulling oars on a rowing machine. Jogging on a treadmill. Frying his naked ass on a tanning bed.

Quick cut to his bored wife, Althea (Estelle Parsons), in a separate bedroom. She stares vacantly into space as she keeps count of her husband's clumsy foot-falls. In contrast to his wife's doughy color, Gerber's skin looks unnatural. His color is what "the pork-colored...white niggers" might've looked like in George Schuyler's 1930s' diddy-bop novel *Black No More*—looking for all the world as if he had been thrown into a vat of corrosive *skin-bleachener.*

The truth is—and this is Melvin's joke—Jeff Gerber isn't white. He's "flesh tone." The color of a Band-Aid.

The joke is well-deserved. Blackface's insult was whitey's attempt to steal our skin and wear our hides like an antebellum Ed Gein acting out mommy issues. Or, as Frederick Douglass said, "... the filthy scum of white society, who have stolen from us a complexion denied to them by nature, in which to make money, and pander to the corrupt taste of their white fellow citizens."

"Flesh tone" has the splotchy look of Vitiligo on black and brown skin. Certainly most any black child growing up in Melvin's generation asked *Why is the color of a Band-Aid called "flesh tone" when it doesn't match the "tone" of my flesh?*

Now, I have no idea how often children in this age of multicultural Band-Aids and Kumbaya crayons are confronted with this issue but "flesh tone" was definitely a thing during my time in elementary school. As a matter of fact, after scrutinizing one of my crayon drawings, the face of my kindergarten teacher burst into all kinds of purple.

Is this what we look like to you?!! Are you colorblind?!!

My crime? I chose the wrong color crayon and colored white people orange. Apparently, the correct answer was *no* crayon at all. Draw an outline and leave it *blank*. White people, apparently, are the pigment of the paper they're drawn on, not a piece of citrus.

I was sent to the principal's office, who in turn, sent me to the school's resident psychologist. Color her *gray*.

But I digress.

Watermelon Man was written by Herman Raucher—a Brooklyn-born, Mad Ave whyte-dude with a foundation in theater and early television. He scripted *Sweet November*; *Can Heironymous Merkin Ever Forget Mercy Humppe and Find True Happiness?* (with Anthony "Candy Man" Newley); *Ode to Billy Joe*; the autobiographical *Summer of '42* and *Class of '44*. With the exception of *Watermelon Man*, I've not seen a single frame of any of these films (despite the popularity of *Summer of '42* during my high school years). It was Raucher's deep annoyance with the hypocrisy of white liberalism that led to his idea for *Watermelon Man* (fair enough. Irks me, too).

The title, too, is from a track on Herbie Hancock's 1962 album debut, *Takin' Off*. It's been covered by a host of artists—Mongo Santamaria; Count Basie; Quincy Jones; Xavier Cugat; King Curtis; Maynard Ferguson; Jimmy McGriff; Sly & Robbie—but perhaps the version most significant to Melvin Van Peebles is by singer Oscar Brown, Jr. The song is sung. Brown supplied lyrics to the instrumental. And delivered those lyrics not only with great musicality but as a commanding storyteller in the manner of a street peddler. It's classic *griot*.

Watermelon!

Pretty little housewife
Let me sell you one.

Red, ripe watermelon

If you want to treat
your husband right...

Watermelon!

Know what to give him
when he's home tonight...

Melvin, on the other hand, introduced himself to black radio-consciousness nationally by presenting his calling card: *Brer Soul*, his debut studio album in 1968. What Van Peebles achieved has characterized his work throughout his career: he told story through song; working with blues song-forms (or what guitarist Michael Gregory Jackson's older brother, Bruce, called "talkin' spook music"). He was inspired by a component of German opera called *sprechstimme*—a form of vocalizing midway between singing and speaking guided by musical rhythms. Additionally, it was the blackened John Howard Griffin's experience in the cracka south that played an important role in Raucher's screenplay.

In *Watermelon Man*, Jeff believes his skin condition is a consequence of hours under a sunlamp. It's actually the soy sauce added to his daily "healthy drink" given to him by none other than Mantan Moreland.

In *Black Like Me*, Griffin, after recovering from blindness due to a war-related head injury, imagines what life would be like as an itinerant black man in cracka south (whose handiman skills are the true original of rock-n-roll. Y'know, 'cause of those rare 78s he cut in the '30s. And the white kids blowing weed with him in the tool shed). He scored some cash from the publishers of *Sepia* to support his *How Crackas Be Treated If They Waz Niggaz* tour. Then bathed under black-light rays and popped assorted non-bleaching pills, inducing the mutation of his skin's pigmentation. The pre-wigger trendsetter was years ahead of pill-popping hippies under black-light (who, unfortunately, didn't successfully repeat the results of Griffin's skin-seasoning experiment).

In the sixties, apparently, cocktail parties were a-twitter with tales of riotous negroes and Griffith's modernist take on *Daddy Rice*. Raucher was probably set off by a situation very much like this one. I can relate. I once attended such an affair in the gated-community of Calabasas, CA. I was the sole guest of a distinctive hue (with the exception, of course, of the aproned ladies ladling spiceless macaroni salad onto paper plates) and it was Martin Luther King's birthday. To mark the occasion, a woman walked up and told me what her daughter had learned in school that day.

"Mommy," the woman's little girl had said, "did you know when Martin Luther King was a little boy, Ronald McDonald wouldn't sell him a cheeseburger because he was African-American?"

"What do you think of that?" the woman asked. She was deadly serious.

"He should've gone to Burger King and ordered a Whopper."

"*No! No! No!* Really, what do you think? You're *black*!"

"I'm sorry, I'm still thinking about the shenanigans I witnessed in front of your house..."

"What shenanigans?!!"

And I tell her.

I had stepped outside to smoke, standing on the welcome mat with a leaf of rolling paper and a pinch of tobacco. As I'm rolling the cigarette, I checked out the neighborhood, thinking it looked like Edward Scissorhands' pastel-colored suburbia.

An O.J. Simpson Ford Bronco rolls past. It stops. Backs up. Idles.

A cabin full of prep-school-suited teens blasting high-volume gangsta rap locked eyes with me. I stared back, blinked a few times and exhaled a trail of cigarette smoke. I was sure they were going to ask if they could score some weed.

"Nigger!!!"

The "crew" of prep-school gangstas burst into guffaws and the Bronco sped off.

Did they just confuse me with a hip-hop sneaker mogul and his fat-assed white woman new to the neighborhood?

When I finished my tale, the silicone bags embedded in the woman's cheeks ruptured and sprayed globules of clotted fat in the air as her faced warped into a Cthulian tangle.

"On Martin Luther King Day?!!?"

With dragonfly agility, she darted from the room. She screamed her home was under attack by gangs of unruly teenage eugenicists. Suddenly, the walls thundered with the din of tramping feet, self-righteous cursing, slamming doors, crashing chandeliers and revving engines. Werewolf-like, her guests had turned into a mob of angry villagers with torches raised high, ready to immolate anyone who *dared* defile the legacy of that holiest of black men, *Dr. Martin Luther King!*

Conversely, I soberly assessed the situation. My wisest choice was a table at Jumbo's Clown Room in West Hollywood.

With *Watermelon Man*, Melvin didn't materialize from behind a veil of swirling cigar-smoke and walk on to a movie set. His career began, curiously enough, with a children's book. It was titled *The Big Heart*. Set in the city of San Francisco, it describes Melvin's routine as a cable car driver through his daily journal entries and a series of black-and-white photos.

One afternoon a passenger climbed into his car, saw his book and browsed its pages. "*Ooooooh!!!* This is a marvelous book! How did you do this?"

"I put some biography here and a photograph there..."

"It's just like a film! You're a director!"

The passenger's observant comment was Melvin's clarifying moment. He followed *The Big Heart* with *Three Pickup Men for Herrick* and *Sunlight*, two film shorts. His films were screened in NYC for an audience of finger-popping Maynard G. Kreb cineastes. Someone approached him afterwards and said they wanted to arrange to have his films exhibited in France. So, in 1959, Melvin relocated to Holland with his family. He found employment with the Dutch National Theater and divorced his wife.

Impressed by his two short films, the founder of the Cinematheque Francaise, Henri Langlois, invited Melvin to the city of lights, where his films were applauded and his pockets unrewarded. His French hosts left him on the streets blowing a kazoo for his supper.

In Paris, Melvin hung with the black expat crowd with persons like Chester Himes (whom he translated for the French edition of *Mad*). He did cloak and dagger investigative journalism. He interviewed Malcolm X and published five novels. His last served as the basis of his first feature film with a grant from the French Cinema Center, *The Story of a Three-Day Pass*. So impressive was its debut, the film was selected by the French to represent the country in the San Francisco Film Festival in 1967.

Meanwhile, Columbia Pictures acquired the rights to *Watermelon Man*. But rather than shoot with director Stanley Kramer, featuring a golly-wogged Spencer Tracy and Tony Curtis in the Mantan Moreland role, they chose the latest French New Wave auteur (it was the sixties): Melvin Van Peebles. It would be his first and last studio-financed project.

Watching the film for the first time in fifty-odd years, I opened by saying *Watermelon Man* irritated the fuck out of me. The first three-quarters of the film looked and sounded *corny*. Godfrey Cambridge plays Jeff Gerber without grooves—loud, goofy, oblivious and overbearing with zero subtlety. A human *annoyance*. The music is a reinvention of ragtime by John Phillip Sousa while on a raging drunk with Carl Stalling in a scrap-metal yard.

It all seemed rather odd until I remembered reading Melvin had conflicts with Herman Raucher, the screenwriter. And then it became obvious. Melvin *hated* the story.

He explains Raucher's original script this way—initially titled *The Night the Sun Came Out on Happy Hollow Lane*, the white Jeff Gerber wakes up one night, goes to the bathroom and sits down to shit. He stands up and the audience is slapped in the face with a full-shot of a sparkling black ass. The script ends, according to Melvin, with Jeff going to the bathroom to take another shit. He stands and his ass is a sparkling bubble-gum pink. The End. Roll credits.

In Melvin's mind, the script equates black people with *shit*.

Clearly, the film's irritable aspects are Melvin expressing both his disgust and subverting its script's original premise. What else did you expect him to do? This is a man once honored by the minister of defense for The Black Panther Party, the late Huey P. Newton, with an entire issue of the party's newspaper devoted to *Sweet Sweetback's Baadasssss Song*.

Raucher retaliated by adapting his script and publishing *Watermelon Man* as a novel. This, apparently, was meant to block Melvin from making good on a clause in his contractual agreement.

The film literally shifts tone with a song (or what I referred to earlier as *sprechstimme*). The color palette darkens. The parody of whitey's sub-vaudevillian humor ends. Melvin's griot kicks in and the mood is somber. Jeff develops character.

Jeff arrives home to his wife accompanied by the plaintive music of a flute. Althea, his wife, stands patiently, reservedly, in the living room, attempting to mask how frightened she feels. The phone rings. Althea tells him not to answer it. He does.

Move out, Nigger!

Jeff calmly puts down the phone. *They've been calling all day*, Althea explains.

She offers him a meal and they walk into the kitchen. She serves him a black-dotted slice of watermelon. This causes an argument marked by the sort of insensitivity that sometimes occurs in salt-n-pepper couplings.

Retiring to the bedroom, Jeff shows an interest in Althea's affections. It's the first time he's done so in the course of this story. He attempts cuddling. She curls up on the opposite side of the bed. Clearly, she ain't feelin' that jungle fever.

The gulf between his desire and her buried disdain is telling and poignant. It's a declaration of who they are. It clarifies the emptiness of their love. And it reveals how they are blinkered by the cultural mirage of race.

The following evening, the neighbors stop by after Jeff's long hard day shoveling at the garbage dump. Beefy white men with faces bloated by alcohol. They crowd the living room, establishing dominance. The men say they have the backing of three banks and propose buying his home. It would be best for the neighborhood's overall sense of financial well-being if he vacated the premises.

Jeff stands before them respectfully, in suit and tie, and, well, *Jeffs* (but done so with self respect). They offer him forty k. He walks away with one-hundred grand. Althea is upset by the transaction. She blurts—

You took advantage of them because you're COLORED! They were our *friends!*

There's the rub. She is blind to her neighbors' unfair treatment of her husband, only seeing how his trickster's response was disadvantageous to both her and her neighbors. Throughout it all, despite Jeff's heartfelt overtures, Althea's whiteness trumps love.

Melvin underscores this moment by following it with another. Jeff gyrates under a billowing sheet with an office co-worker—a French-speaking floozie with a raw dumpling of a body. She drizzles with *White Castle's* burger-bag greasiness. During a post-coital conversation, with a soft-spoken eloquence, Jeff explains he wants to be loved for who he is, not because he is a Negro.

He also calls her "a big blonde bigot." Suddenly, in her mind, Jeff, a "polite negro," is transformed into a black bastard, a nigger, a rapist...

By jove! I think you've got it! He welcomes her to America. And leaves.

In his suburban home, he is greeted by a note of apology without explanation. His wife and kids have left him. He is now alone in the world with a black man's skin.

His nights are seen in montage, signaled only by his suit's changing patterns. Neon and nightclubs. Bawdy brown girls. Police harassment and barroom shakedowns. Melvin appears and paints Jeff's independence on a door.

In the end, an instrument symbolizing subservience, a mop, is his *weapon*.

An Interview with Actress Donna Dubrow (Guest Starring Sandra Rusch)

Donna Dubrow's acting career began and ended with *Watermelon Man*, in which she played the receptionist at Jeff Gerber's office. Dubrow later produced a number of films, including *Medicine Man*, *The Favor*, and *The Last Innocent Man*. The role of the receptionist wasn't a big role by any stretch of the imagination, but again, only a handful of people who worked on *Watermelon Man* are still alive.

Sandra Rusch is Dubrow's sister and a one-time girlfriend of Melvin Van Peebles. Rusch just happened to be present when Dubrow and I had our phone interview, so she hopped on the line to discuss Van Peebles and the film.

ANDREW J. RAUSCH: *How did you land the role in* Watermelon Man*?*

DONNA DUBROW: I should have you talk to my sister. My sister and Melvin were boyfriend and girlfriend. He came back from France after having done *Story of a Three-Day Pass*. I was trying to act. Just do commercials or something to occupy myself, you know? I had a two-year-old son. So, he said, "Do you want a little part in the movie?" To be crude, I used to say to people, "My sister fucked the director and I got the job."

AR: *What do you remember about the experience of being on set?*

DD: I had been on a few movie sets before, you know? But it was the typical kind of movie thing. It was a Columbia Picture, I believe. I think we shot something on the lot. The idea, if it had been done right, was sort of game-changing at its time. I think everyone was afraid to really do what should have been done, you know? Which could be done now, which was the idea that you have a racist white man becoming a black. But it was a fascinating idea.

AR: *When you say the "way it should have been done," what do you mean? With more bite? Less comedy?*

DD: Yeah. I mean if it had really been done... Godfrey Cambridge was... I guess at that time he was a well-known comedian. If you were going to do it, you should do it head-on. They just kind of walked around things. Just like them fucking. At the time, I don't think Columbia really had their heart in it as far as promoting it and really doing much with it. It could have been quite fascinating. Those were not exactly liberal times in the world. Actually, compared to now, they probably were.

AR: *Isn't that terrible?*

DD: *We've gone backwards in fifty years or how ever long it's been. My sister Sandra is here. She's downstairs. Let's put her on the phone with you, too, okay?*

AR: *Okay.*

DD: She may remember. What was the name of the other producer? The other one besides John Bennett? Is he still alive?

AR: *His name was Leon Mirell. He passed away.*

DD: That's right. He was a lovely man.

Her sister, Sandra, gets on the phone.

SANDRA RUSCH: What I remember is that it was the first time a black director was getting the opportunity to make a film.

DD: It should have been game-changing if it had been done right. Everybody kind of stepped around it. They hired Melvin and they stepped around the whole subject matter and what they were really doing with it. I watched it again yesterday for my birthday. It's a terrible movie, but I saw my whatever it was... My two lines in it.

AR: *So you both knew Melvin. What do you remember about Melvin? What was he like?*

DD: Oh, my God, we've been in touch with Melvin and the kids forever. [Melvin's son] Mario is still very much a part of our lives.

SR: Melvin was very funny. Iconoclastic and mischievous at the same time. That's how he got away with doing things. He didn't ask, he just went ahead and did things. His breakthrough movie, *Sweet Sweetback*, was a movie where he got to tell it like it was. Melvin was very talented. He was talented in many areas besides just film directing; he could write and act in theatre, he did poetry, he could draw—

DD: He became the first black member of the New York Stock Exchange. He did it on a bet. Someone proposed a bet about him getting on the New York Stock Exchange. Then he wrote a book called *Bold Money* about the stock exchange stuff.

AR: *It is interesting to compare* Watermelon Man *to* Sweet Sweetback's Baadasssss Song *because he made that film exactly the way he wanted with no interference. While I think* Sweet Sweetback *is a pretty rudimentary film, I think it feels much more genuine.*

DD: With *Sweetback* he put up his own money. And Bill Cosby gave him fifty thousand dollars.

SR: It was his story and his film, where *Watermelon Man* was a studio production.

DD: And he had just come back from France where he'd made *Story of a Three-Day Pass*, which had gotten awards.

AR: *Did Melvin tell you anything about the way he felt he was being treated by the studio? What do you remember about that?*

SR: He just ignored them and went ahead and did what he wanted to do, and didn't tell them anything about what he was doing. He just did it.

DD: I don't think it was a great experience. He never wanted to do another studio movie after that. That's why he went off and did his own thing.

AR: *What do you remember about Godfrey Cambridge? Did you get to talk to him?*

DD: He was okay. He wasn't particularly approachable. He certainly wasn't funny on set. I don't remember him being funny for someone who was a comedian.

SR: I don't think he was very political either. I don't think this was his typical project. I think it was a Hollywood part, so he took it.

AR: *I've been told that Melvin and Godfrey didn't get along very well. What do you remember about that?*

SR: I don't remember that.

DD: I don't remember it, but I wouldn't question it either. I'm sure it was probably true. Melvin and Godfrey were different. Godfrey was absolutely happy playing a white man. Melvin was fully who he was.

AR: *Looking back on it, what are your thoughts on being involved with* Watermelon Man*?*

DD: I had such a small part. I mean, it was fun for me to be in a movie that was going to be a Hollywood movie. It was all positive. Everybody was very nice. Melvin was always very nice to me, of course. I think around that time Mario was staying with me part of the time. And Mario was what? Ten years old at that time?

BIOGRAPHER MICHAEL H. PRICE TALKS ABOUT MANTAN MORELAND

Michael H. Price is an actor and cultural historian. He has written a number of cinema-themed books, including the *Forgotten Horrors* series. Most notably for the purposes of this book, Price is the author of the Mantan Moreland biography, *Mantan the Funnyman: The Life and Times of Mantan Moreland.* Moreland's contributions to cinema, and more importantly, black cinema, are often overlooked. And perhaps worse, his contributions are *misunderstood.* Since Moreland made one of his final screen appearances in *Watermelon Man* (in the memorable role of the "Counterman"), I reached out to Price to discuss the late actor, his legacy, and *Watermelon Man.*

ANDREW J. RAUSCH: *For the people who don't know much about Mantan Moreland, could you talk a little bit about who he was and what his legacy is?*

MICHAEL H. PRICE: He was a Louisiana-born natural comedian. He seems to have quietly obtained the nickname "Mantan the Funnyman" as a child. One of his grandmothers gave him that nickname. He was born under the family name of Broadnaks. His father was a citizen of Monroe, Louisiana, who had a brief affair with Mantan's mother. So the child was basically raised by his grandmother. He developed this technique of making people laugh very early on. So the grandmother made up this rhyme about "Mantan the Funnyman." And it stuck with him. He took the family name of his father, Moreland.

He ran away from home in his early teens and connected with a minstrel troupe. That led to circus work with the Hagenbeck-Wallace Circus. Among his colleagues was a clown named Red

Skelton. So he basically worked his way up to Broadway and then from Broadway into the movies. Tentatively beginning in the early 1930s in Warner Bros' Long Island studio. He did a short comedy with a partner, but he didn't breakthrough to the movies until the later 1930s, doing what were basically comedy relief parts. He did Westerns, comedies, spooky comedies. Most people know him today for an early-Forties' picture called *King of the Zombies*, where he basically steals the show away from the white guy heroes. Mantan is the one who spots the danger, tries to alert people, gets resoundingly ignored, and then finally gets in the last word. One of the most bizarre closing lines in the movies; he says, "If there's anything I wouldn't want to be twice, zombies is both of them!"

The trick was, Mantan had an actor/writer contract with Monogram Pictures, a very tiny studio. The contract required no original scenarios, but rather his ability to improvise while shooting. So he was basically writing his roles while he was enacting them. Mantan worked for most of the major studios, doing small parts, and was a bonafide star at Monogram Pictures. He even named his homestead in Hollywood "Monogram Ranch."

He wrapped up his Hollywood career playing the chauffeur-turned-colleague to Charlie Chan in the Mongram series.

AR: *I interviewed director Jack Hill last year. He told me that at the time he cast Mantan Moreland in* Spider Baby, *there was a bit of a backlash from the black community regarding the stereotypical type of characters he was associated with playing. Obviously, this was before* Watermelon Man, *but would you say that assessment is accurate?*

MP: There was no stereotype in Mantan. He ridiculed the concept of dialogue, although he spoke in his natural Louisiana drawl. There's a series of pictures that he made at Monogram with a young Irish actor named Frankie Darrow, where they played buddies; a mixed buddy team. This was generations before *Lethal Weapon*. They played amateur sleuths in their various pictures. There's one scene in the Monogram pictures with Frankie Darrow where they're getting ready to rehearse a comedy routine for an audition, and Mantan turns to Frankie and says, "You don't expect me to be speakin' no dialect, do you?" So, he was inverting and ridiculing the stereotypes, even while he was basically being accused of perpetuating the stereotypes.

He was unique among black Hollywood players in that he did not subscribe to the subservient image. He talked back, and he took a pro-active role in his characters. The image of Mantan is unique. He is not of the Lincoln Perry Stepin Fetchit school of acting. He exhibited bravery. He also exhibited the courage to scram when the going got threatening. But he was ready to stand and fight if need be. You can trace that all through his portrayals, especially at Monogram. He plays an equal, more or less, to Shemp Howard in a Universal picture from that period called *The Strange Case of Dr. RX*. I don't know if you've seen the picture, but it's almost a classic Stooge routine. It bolsters the story I was told by Moe Howard during the early Seventies, that Shemp had recommended Mantan for a third Stooge role if anything should happen to Shemp. By that time, Monogram had ended its Charlie Chan series.

There was, quite frankly, a blacklisting by the NAACP, which basically scared the studios off of working with Mantan; as putting him in such a role as Shemp Howard had recommended. It became problematic for him. He was suffering from a diabetic condition, still eager to work, still thwarted by the studio blacklist. So, he basically went back to working the comedy club circuit. He had outlived a couple of team partners in that area, so he kept hooking up with new partners such as Nipsey Russell. He basically just kept on keepin' on insofar as circumstances would allow. It was the likes of Jack Hill and Melvin Van Peebles that recognized that brilliance and did what they could to bring Mantan back into something near the spotlight.

AR: *As you said, unfairly or not, Mantan did get lumped in with Stepin Fetchit, even though their approaches were different. Mantan was trying to satirize the stereotypes while Stepin Fetchit seemed to lean into it and embraced it. Obviously, Mantan got stuck with an unfair label. Why do you feel it is that people were quick to attach that label onto him, and why do you think it stuck?*

MP: No sense of humor. As Carl Reiner and many others have said, "Satire dies on Saturday night." People don't get it. That's why publications like *Mad* magazine ran afoul of complaints of irresponsible storytelling. That's why Robert Crumb got busted in San Francisco during the underground comics days for satirizing pornography. That same sort of puritanical attitude...basically it's retrograde. It's reactionary.

AR: *As they say, "nuance is everything." But I think, very often nuance is lost on people.*

MP: Yes. Nuance is a dangerous path to tread, and yet it's the only honest approach. There's a bit of subversion there, and it's constructive subversion.

AR: *Obviously, Melvin Van Peebles recognized what Mantan Moreland was doing and sought to utilize that in his character in* Watermelon Man.

MP: Mantan had the best double-take in the business. That's even including masters of the double take, including Oliver Hardy and Edgar Kennedy. His familiarity with Godfrey Cambridge's character in *Watermelon Man* is such that when Cambridge shows up as another person altogether, Mantan's double-take is in overdrive. He's kind of a small Greek chorus in *Watermelon Man.*

AR: *There's a story in the liner notes booklet to the new Melvin Van Peebles Criterion box set about Melvin advising Mantan, "Don't make it clear that we're saying fuck you." That's a very funny and telling line. Because that's a lot of what Melvin was doing—he was trying to sneak in things to make the film one thing while the studio thought he was making another. Do you have any thoughts on that?*

MP: It's just amazing that Melvin snuck that film past the suits at Columbia. [Laughs.] Basically, that's my thought on it. It's a bracing film. Jarring. The finale of *Watermelon Man* is straight out of the Malcolm X playbook. It's quite astonishing how he pulled that off. It's far from a flawless picture. The makeup on Cambridge is not entirely convincing. Michael Weldon once said that Cambridge looked like a black guy who sneezed into a bowl of flour. But there's a conviction in that leading performance that is endemic to the whole film. It's like, "This is a film that *believes* what it has to say," even though sometimes the telling of that story is a bit clunky. But then he musters his militance there toward the end, then comes out with a statement as opposed to a finale.

AR: *With the lead character, Jeff Gerber, Melvin and Godfrey Cambridge are very much satirizing the image of white people in the same way that Mantan was satirizing the image of black people. I find that interesting and quite funny.*

MP: It's almost a valedictory performance for Mantan. Not quite, because he did other work. But the reciprocity of satire...I'm hard put to think of a more emphatic film in that regard.

AR: *Since Mantan Moreland and Godfrey Cambridge were both comedians and did a lot of stage work, I wondered if you knew of any kind of relationship or interactions between them?*

MP: Not to my knowledge. It would have been a natural. The two actors play off of one another like a comedy team. Even though they're not officially bonded as characters, there is a bond that transcends the disorientation that Mantan feels. It's a very sympathetic reaction that he pulls, and his reaction in turn becomes a forward thinking observation. He's concerned, he has empathy, and yet he's like, "What's going on here?" You almost expect him to launch into one of his signature Monogram-type lines.

AR: *Is there any record of what Montan thought about the film?*

MP: I know that his daughter Marcella, since deceased, she has reminisced... We didn't go into detail in the Mantan book because that would have been a tangent, but he recalled it fondly and primarily with gratitude for getting the work. I'm paraphrasing, but she said he felt he was back on top for a little while.

HOW TO EAT WATERMELON IN WHITE COMPANY (AND ENJOY IT) FILMMAKER JOE ANGIO

by Rob St. Mary

Joe Angio has produced, directed, and edited (with Joel Cohen) the short documentaries *More Than a Game* and *Feast of Fools*. For his first feature-length film, Angio set his sights on documenting the life and career of Melvin Van Peebles. The filmmaker then followed Van Peebles around the globe for nearly a decade. Angio's documentary, *How to Eat Your Watermelon in White Company (and Enjoy It)*, was released to critical acclaim and was awarded both the Jury Award and Audience Award at the 2006 Biografilm Festival in Italy.

ROB ST. MARY: *What brought you to the idea of making a film about Melvin Van Peebles?*

JOE ANGIO: I sort of came to his story through a side entrance. I'm friends with— Remember that part in the film where there are these two guys who are stock traders talking about Melvin's life on Wall Street? Those guys are both friends of mine; former roommates at different times. And the one guy, Brett Nichols, he was actually Melvin's clerk on the floor of the American Stock Exchange. First black optioner on the New York Stock Exchange. That's [Melvin's] claim to fame on that. And Brett used to tell me all these stories about Melvin. I'm going years back here, I'm talking like the mid-80s, okay? I'd heard of *Sweetback*, but I'd never seen it. So he would tell me all these stories about Melvin. You know, running with Melvin and the music he'd done and a playwright and he started running marathons at forty, just on and on and on. So, finally I watched *Sweetback*, and I'm sure you— It's funny, on your site I actually read a little bio of you, about your dad showing you *Watermelon Man* and *A Clockwork Orange*. So, that's like me watching *Sweetback*— I probably sort of had the same reaction as anyone who saw *Sweetback* for the first time. Like, what the fuck is this thing, you know? So, I got intrigued with him. Just from hearing all of Brett's stories, he became alive in my mind as a potential subject for a film.

But it wasn't until many, many years later—more than ten years later—that I actually met him and proposed the idea to him. So, I'd been sort of stalking him from afar for like thirteen years. Much of it pre-internet age, so I couldn't even find the stuff online. When I first moved to New York, I was going up to the Performing Arts Library up at Lincoln Center and getting information from there, whatever I could find on him, and I sort of built this dossier and had this whole proposal for a film before I finally approached him.

RSM: *What was the process like when you first sat down and said, "Hey, I'd like do this film on your career and all the odd things you've done over your life"?*

JA: Well, it's kind of interesting in a way because, as I just described to you, I had built this...all this background and research for so long, but I hadn't reached out to him in any way. At the time, I'd only made two short films. A short film and an hour-long documentary, neither of which had gotten to a wide audience. They'd gotten into festivals and on various TV channels here and there, but I had no name to speak of. And I'm a white guy. I kind of thought, why isn't Spike Lee doing this film? Or the Hudlin brothers or someone like that?

My friend Michael Solomon, who later became my partner on this film and the producer of it— We were having lunch one day. I also had this kind of parallel magazine editing career I'd fallen into when I moved to New York from Chicago. So I had a couple film projects that were in some nebulous state of trying to find money, but my heart wasn't completely in them, coupled with me sort of having a full-time job for the first time in my life and actually making some money. At lunch one day, Michael asked me, "What's the deal? Are you gonna make another film?" Like I said, he had hooked me up with the producer on this other film that was just kind of withering on the vine. I was like, "Yeah, there's that, but the film I really wanna make is on Melvin Van Peebles." His jaw kind of dropped, and he was like, "Joe, I know Melvin really well." And Michael's a good friend. We'd known each other for years. It had just never come up. We'd never talked about this.

So, to make kind of a long story short, from what first started as Michael being my liaison to get to Melvin—because his thing was always kind of, "This is Melvin. You've gotta come correct with Melvin. For him to take you seriously, you're gonna have to have money behind you to do this right." And whenever I went out to try to get the money, they were saying, "Melvin's onboard, right?" It was kind of a vicious circle; a catch-22. So finally, after about a year of futile efforts to raise the money for the film, I was like, we've just got to get Melvin onboard. I asked Michael if he would want to come on as a producer, and he said, "Absolutely." So he then brokered the introduction. And I hadn't really appreciated just how well Michael actually knew Melvin. So here when I finally met him in March of '98, I'd been sort of sitting on this thing for a number of years before that. In my mind, as long as Melvin hadn't said no, the project was still alive. It was one of the most nerve-wracking days of my life because we're sitting in this booth and I'm all prepared for my spiel of what I'm gonna say to Melvin, and I didn't even have to utter a word. We were sitting in this diner, and he looked at me, and he turned to Michael and said, "Your friend Michael Solomon has had my back for years and helped me out of a lot of jams. I read your proposal and he vouches for you. That's good enough for me. I'll do it." I didn't have to convince him at all. It was that sudden and that easy. And it was all based on the trust he'd had with Michael.

RSM: *That's pretty amazing. I was gonna say, he comes across in interviews and, obviously, the film you did as a very independent guy who is strong in his opinions, strong in his art and life. How was he to work with and sit down and actually put it together with?*

JA: That's the thing, like I was saying, he doesn't suffer fools gladly. [Laughs.] It ended up being great. I know Melvin has had some run-ins with people that he's had relationships with before that aren't there anymore. I think the fact that it was Michael and I, and Michael had the trust of a friend and someone who was close to him, that I could come in with some distance; keep some journalistic distance and objectivity about it. And since I was the director and had creative control of it, and Michael was facilitating making it happen as a producer... We really were on all the shoots together. We were kind of a two-man band on the whole production. So, it was a very nice, really good dynamic. I guess I just never did anything to really piss him off other than step in his shot one time when we were shooting and filming his movie in France. I was kind of on the side and I stepped into his shot, and I thought he was gonna tear my head off. [Laughs.] But other than that, I can't even think of a testy moment. You know, maybe sometimes he was tired, but he was a trooper. He was always game. It just went on so long, you know? A lot of it was due to some garden variety independent filmmaking reasons, but most of it was really due to... I also had a full-time job the entire time I made the film, so that had some to do with it. You know, eight years. It literally coincided, eight years, almost to the day, of when I was the editor at *Time Out New York* magazine. We started shooting the film on the Saturday after my first week there. I left the week it opened at Film Forum in New York.

But the thing is, the very first thing I shot in the film was him rehearsing with the band that would become Roadkill that we showed in the music section. You know, he's singing the Sheryl Crow song, "All I Wanna Do (Is Have Some Fun)," and he's trying to teach the piano player in the next room the words. That was the very first thing we shot, and I thought, "Oh great, this is our ending. Here's what he's doing now. He's going out with his band and he's going to perform at these clubs." Then the next year, he's going to France to shoot his first movie in fifteen years. And then I was like, "Oh great, there's our ending. We've gotta shoot that!" [Laughs.] He just kept doing things like that for the next five, six years. Like, "Ah, we've gotta shoot that! There's our ending!"

That whole thing he was doing with Isaac Julien. We don't mention Isaac Julien in the film, but the whole making of the sculpture of him was for this exhibition and opening of this film this British artist and filmmaker Isaac Julien was doing on blaxploitation. In it, he encounters this replica, this inanimate statue of Melvin, who comes to life. So they had to create this statue. And we shot that whole process of making that from the casting to the actual creation of the sculpture. And that became sort of this gift from heaven that fell on our lap and, as you know, became a sort of through-line that carries the film.

RSM: *He's had such a varied career. I mean, you talked about your friends who were stock brokers, he had Broadway plays, he had films, all this stuff. When you went through and started to reach out to the various people that he had been in touch with over his lifetime and doing the work, what was the reaction? Did you get doors slammed in your face, or did you get people going, "Yeah, yeah, I'd love to talk about him"?*

JA: Oh yeah, totally that! No doors slammed in our face at all. If he's burned any bridges, which I'm sure he has over the years, I didn't know who those people were; we didn't talk to them. No one we spoke with had anything really bad to say about him. That could also be, as an artist in his older years now, that people remember him more fondly and warmly than some of the battles he was fighting when *Sweetback* was being made and stuff like that.

RSM: *You said you went and you read all these books and had to do all this research before you put the proposal together. When you were making the film itself, what were some of the things that came up that were a total surprise to you? Something that you learned about him that you didn't know?*

JA: The music stuff was the big revelation. I didn't know that he had had the influence and impact that he had. It's almost conventional wisdom. You hear people like Gil Scott-Heron and the Last Poets are the linchpins—the precursors for any rap artist. It kind of goes back to them as saying they're the primary key influences. And to have them go back and say it was Melvin. And hand in hand with that, to find out how he actually taught himself to make music... That was pretty amazing. Which we learned that's how he did everything. We had the story from my two friends who were the traders—he made up his own system for trading down there. He'd never made a film, but he kind of figured out and learned how to make films but he didn't know any of the technical processes of doing so. So, that was one of them. There were a few of them. But to me, music was definitely one of the biggest revelations. I knew of the music background, but I knew literally nothing about it. Then actually going and hearing those records. *Brer Soul* is a great record. I love that record.

RSM: *When it comes to the music, that obviously includes* Watermelon Man. *He did that soundtrack and the film's theme song, "Love, That's America." In his conversations with you, when you were talking about* Watermelon Man, *do you remember how he came on to that project? How Columbia Pictures said, "Yeah, come to our studio and make this film"?*

JA: Yes and no. I'd hate to be the final source on this, because yes, he told me, but I might get it wrong. There was one story Melvin talked about a few times, which was, when he came back to America after making his first film in France, *La Permission*. This film was vetted at the San Francisco International Film Festival. I think it won Best Film. And he was getting all these offers. When he came back, people didn't think he was American, let alone black. So, he was getting all these offers to direct films. As Melvin tells it, he wasn't going to accept the job. I never quite understood it. It seems a little convoluted to me. But, as he put it, he thought Hollywood, speaking broadly, capital "H," wanted to hire a black director basically to set them up to fail, to then prove their superiority, like "Ah, see, we shouldn't have done this." To do it on some kind of project they weren't going to entrust a big budget. And Melvin just kept refusing these offers because he believed he was being set up to fail for them to prove this point. So, he didn't do anything right away.

Remember, he comes back to America... He makes *La Permission*— Help me out on the dates if you're fact checking this stuff. I'm really rusty. [Laughs.]

RSM: *That's in the last sixties. That's like '67.*

JA: And *Watermelon Man* is '70. So he does those three records for A&M in the interim, you know? He comes back with this triumph to the States as a filmmaker, and doesn't make films. He goes into music, and somehow finagles this deal with A&M Records [and] he makes three records. And in that time, eventually, the script for *Watermelon* got to him. And that's when, I guess he figured enough time had passed or whatever, that now there was something he could do that he felt he could do justice to that he would take on. But there's that interim there where he claims he was being offered films and turning them down, for that reason—the reason I don't fully understand as he described it.

RSM: *It's interesting if you look at it in that period because there are not really a lot of prominent black folks in that era (in the late 1960s). Really the only one you could probably point to is Sidney Poitier, right?*

JA: Right.

RSM: *So one can understand where he's like, "Alright, this is a little suspect if the only model we have is Sidney Poitier."*

JA: Same, too, on stage. It's the same thing, which they allude to, he and his producer on stage, Emanuel Azenberg; there was black theater, but that was like *A Raisin in the Sun* and those kind of things. There wasn't a real kind of *black* theater.

RSM: *The one story that he tells, and I was wondering if there was more to or if you can kind of explain it a bit, where he said that he got the script and he told the studio, "Oh, yeah, I'll do this," and then changed it.*

JA: That's the ending. Yeah, because the ending, they wanted the whole thing to be like this crazy bad dream sequence, and he wakes up and realizes the folly of his bigotry and he's now like a chastened white man. So, as Melvin tells it, he kind of put out this exaggerated Stepin Fetchit character; "Oh, yessuh, yessuh, I'll shoot the ending that way!" Because they didn't see it in the shooting script. And he never did. But he didn't show it to them until long after they had broken the set and struck it. So they couldn't do anything. They couldn't make him go back and shoot it. It was like, "Oh, yeah, I'll do it, I'll do it," and then he just never shot it that way. He was like, "I wasn't just going to have this guy wake up one day and be okay and everything's sort of okay again."

RSM: *I also heard that he said that the reason he changed the ending was he didn't like the idea that being black was a horrible nightmare.*

JA: Exactly! Exactly! You're right. You just made me think, what was the original ending, whether that was the original ending or what they wanted him [to do]. That's not something I'm really sure of, Robert, whether the script called it that he stayed black or they wanted him to shoot it that way just to see how it played, and he was just like, "I'm not gonna give them that option." As I understand it, it was originally written as such [and] that they wanted this other option. He was like, "No way. If I give them that option, you know what they're going to do with it." But again, you are taxing some distant brain cells here.

RSM: *When you talked to him about this and the fact that he did change the ending, what were they, over at Columbia... How was their reaction, not only with the suits but also the reaction once they put this film out in the theaters?*

JA: I really don't know. I mean, we really used *Watermelon Man* as kind of a transitional thing to get into *Sweetback* and his more personal stuff, you know? We didn't dwell a great deal on *Watermelon Man*. There were so many things we could have made the entire film on, you know, each of these sections of his life.

RSM: *So, talking about the documentary itself, you created it and it took you almost a decade to actually finish the film. As you were saying, it was an eight-year process; even earlier if you go back in terms of putting all the research together. When it came out, how did it work out for you? How did you feel about it, and how did you feel about the reaction to the film?*

JA: I was really happy with it. I think the reactions from the audiences who saw it first at the film festivals and then when it played its limited theatrical runs here in New York and a couple of other places were really gratifying. There are two different parts. On the big broad level, when it's mostly going to film festivals and you're meeting people directly following the screening and you're getting initial feedback, it usually fell into one of two camps, which is "Oh, my God," sort of daunted by his skills and his never say no attitude and like, "I'll never be able to accomplish anything in my life!" But the far greater reaction was that people were getting so inspired, like, "I'm gonna go home and get that novel out of my desk drawer that's been moldering for a couple of years. There's no reason for me not to do anything I want to try to do," after what they've just seen for eighty-five minutes about everything he'd done with all the disadvantages he faced—the obstacles he faced strictly because of his color and upbringing.

But then on another level, there were people—and these were either from contemporaries or people who were really close to him, including Mario, his son—who would say, "Man, I thought I knew everything about Melvin Van Peebles. But I didn't know X was in the theater, or why about the music." They were just really shocked that there was this character they already thought was pretty well-rounded was even more complex and dynamic than they originally thought. As far as Mario, he sat next to me at the Los Angeles Film Festival. And he was hitting my shoulder with the back of his hand throughout the entire movie, sort of going, "Seriously? Are you kidding me?" People were shushing him actually. Afterward, he told me, "Man, there was stuff in there I thought for sure were lies that my dad had told me over the years that you found out to be true and corroborated." So that was kind of gratifying.

RSM: *You know what's funny, a few years later, or maybe about the time that your film came out, Mario made* Badasssss!

JA: That actually preceded the release of our film.

RSM: *I was wondering if in some way there was a connection there, like he knew you were making this, or he was inspired off the fact that you were making something about his dad. How did that come together? Do you know?*

JA: I've wondered the same thing, because we interviewed him well before he ever made that film. It's just that he made his film in a year and we made ours in eight. [Laughs.] I was wondering the same thing when I first heard of *Badasssss!* while he was making it, or maybe he had wrapped it and it hadn't been released yet. I had heard he was making a documentary about his dad and I was like, "*What the fuck?! Are you serious?*" So I was totally unnerved by that. And then when I heard what it was and I actually saw it, I thought, man, this can actually only help. Because I think Sony Classics released it. I thought, this will help to raise some awareness in advance of ours. Whether that worked or not is totally impossible to say.

RSM: *In terms of it, when you saw it, what did you think? Did you think he did a pretty good job?*

JA: I thought so. You know, Mario tends to... Like, whenever we went into our interviews with Mario, who, for the record, was totally gracious and gave us a lot of time—super guy, really nice—but the conversation sort of always came back to Mario. Or I should say Mario kind of always led the conversation back to Mario. So, in the movie I was expecting that. And somehow it didn't. It became this really great homage to his dad. Who am I to say about this? I thought maybe he made it more just to kind of spice up the affect that the opening sex scene from *Sweetback* had on his life, just to give it kind of more dramatic context. But who am I to say that? He would know better than me certainly.

RSM: *Do you think for him maybe it's that he's living in the shadow of his father in some way? An "I've gotta kind of make my own way" kind of thing?*

JA: I think that's plausible, but at the same time, I don't get any sense that he has any resentment or any regret about that. I think he's the first to champion his dad's exploits. And I guess by traditional, or what we in Hollywood would consider measures of success, Mario has far exceeded Melvin, you know? He's made more movies as an actor and as a director. But he hasn't had the lasting impact that Melvin has. And I think Mario has always been really good about giving his dad props for that.

SWEET SWEETBACK AND THE GAUNTLET OF BLACK CINEMA

by Nat Segaloff

Hollywood's relationship with people of color has been an issue ever since moving images were black and white but Nickelodeons audiences weren't. With rare exceptions, people of color in early films were played by whites who "blacked up" to play African-American characters. For various reasons (none of them acceptable today) blacks were not hired to portray themselves.

There were, of course, African-American alternatives to racist Hollywood. Knowledgeable scholarship has explored the history of the Negro Theatre Circuit (*A Separate Cinema*, John Kish and Edward Mapp, NY: Farrar, Straus, Giroux, 1992), the image of black heroes (*From Sambo to Superspade*, David J. Leab, NY: Houghton-Mifflin, 1975), stereotypes (*Toms, Coons, Mulattoes, Mammies, and Bucks*, Donald J. Bogle, NY: Bloomsbury, 2013) and more. Biographies such as Patrick McGilligan's *Oscar Michaeux: The Great and Only* (NY: HarperCollins, 2007) trace this seminal black filmmaker's efforts to counteract Hollywood's racial exclusion.

Little attention has been paid, however, to the fundamental economics of black cinema, something that Melvin van Peebles encountered with his first two films, *The Story of a Three-Day Pass* and *Watermelon Man*, and then confronted head-on in his next film, *Sweet Sweetback's Baadasssss Song*.

I was a movie publicist working with studios and exhibitors in the northeast from 1970 to 1975 and I was privy to a fair amount of inside information from filmmakers, film company executives, and theater owners, most of whom hoped it would never be published. It will do no good to reveal their names now (they're either dead or retired), but their information is useful in describing how the term "black exploitation film" refers less to the movies than to the ritual exploiting of black patrons and filmmakers.

Modern audiences got a sense of those dynamics watching *Dolemite is My Name*, Eddie Murphy's affectionate screen account of blaxploitation film auteur (and tireless self-promoter) Rudy Ray Moore. The filmmakers' skill at conjuring the gauntlet Moore had to run in order to get his film distributed—and its exuberant reception by his intended audience to the bafflement of the white Establishment—was not unique except that he succeeded. In truth, nearly every black-interest film of that period was practically strangled in its crib by a system that wanted black dollars but not black culture.

Without rehashing Hollywood's history of racial stereotyping, from the blackface actors of *The Birth of a Nation* to the stereotyped roles offered to Lincoln Theodore Monroe Andrew Perry (a.k.a. Stepin Fetchit) and Hattie McDaniel to the #OscarSoWhite campaign of 2015, it might be more helpful to do a little math because Hollywood is all about numbers.

In the early 1970s, African-Americans comprised just over eleven percent of the American population, or around 22.6 million people.[1] Many had been migrating from the agricultural South to the industrial north with the expansion of manufacturing in the late 1940s following World War II. Over the next decades they would become the dominant minority group in four-hundred-and-sixty key cities in 1970 and steadily growing.[2]

Hollywood was well aware of this expanding audience but had no firm idea how to attract it to the box office. Major studio releases such as *The Defiant Ones*, *In the Heat of the Night*, *To Sir, With Love*, and *Guess Who's Coming to Dinner* drew crossover audiences largely through the immense appeal of their common star, Sidney Poitier. But it was hard to argue that any of them was about the Black Experience. Crucially, they were made for general (meaning white) audiences, and if blacks drifted in, so much the better.

As always, the indigenous movement began with independent cinema and was spurred by the Civil Rights Struggle. Such notable releases as *Gone Are the Days* (a.k.a. *Purlie Victorious*), *Nothing*

1 "We The Americans: Blacks," U.S. Bureau of the Census, September 1993

2 David Harshbarger and Andre M. Perry, "The Rise of Black-Majority Cities," Brookings Institution, February 26, 2019

But a Man and *The Story of a Three-Day Pass* struck a nerve with black audiences. By no definition could these be called exploitation films, black or otherwise, and they managed to attain bookings in what became known as art-house cinemas in major cities where they drew diverse patrons. Soon Hollywood took notice of this "under-served audience." The problem was that the product craved by the "under-served audience" was at odds with the economics of studio filmmaking.

Simply stated, a film in that time generally had to gross 2.6 times its production cost before starting to show a profit. This was after the deduction, from revenues, of the actual shooting costs, studio overhead, interest on loans, and the myriad "expenses" routinely attached to a movie to keep it from showing a profit on paper.

In the early 1970s, well before today's blockbuster/tentpole era (when films open on thousands of screens and marketing expenses run into the tens of millions), the average studio theatrical feature film cost between one million dollars and three million dollars with less than $150,000 spent on advertising, much of it shared by the theater owner. The picture would open in one of two intown theaters and then, after several weeks, would move to suburban cinemas ("the nabes," or "neighborhoods"). After a few weeks there, it would "go wide" for a week at "a theater or drive-in near you," through a three-tier process known as "clearances." Finally it would languish on a shelf for two years before being sold to TV. The average ticket price during that period was $1.55 to $2.00.[3]

Black-interest films were different. Because it was believed that their audiences were limited to major cities with enough of an African-American population to support them, their production budgets were held down to an amount that could be recouped without suburban play-off and a television sale. Although figures are hard to obtain (and chicanery by distributors was not uncommon), anecdotal evidence is that $200,000 to $350,000 budgets were not unusual.

At first, the major studios weren't interested in "black films" any more than they wanted "Asian films" or "Hispanic films" (although films from China and Mexico did play in theaters in those ethic

3 Source: Motion Picture Association of America

neighborhoods). The box office potential of these pictures wasn't big enough to feed the studio system. Consequently, black-interest films tended to be handled by feisty (and often transitory) indie companies like AIP (American International Pictures), Cinemation, Fanfare, Transview, Cambist, Bryanston, and Dimension (which distributed the original *Dolemites*).

The other hurdle was an almost total absence of black-owned screens. When the major studios owned their own theaters prior to the break-up of their monopolies in 1948, only five percent of U.S. screens drew African-American customers.[4] Although the well-established Columbia Pictures had no trouble getting bookings for *Watermelon Man* in 1970, Melvin Van Peebles faced obstacles when he went looking for bookings for his next film, the independently made *Sweet Sweetback*.

"We were all ready to go. . .all set except for one little thing," he wrote in *The Making of Sweet Sweetback's Baadasssss Song*. "There isn't a black-owned movie chain in America, not even a Negro or a colored one, and all the theaters except two refused to book the picture. Only two theaters in the entire country willing to play the film. But the Man has an Achilles pocketbook and I knew if the film did well all the doors would swing wide. But if the picture bombed for ANY reason, external or not, from an earthquake on down. . .in short, if I didn't come up with a presentable gross, I was dead—typical odds, ghetto-wise."[5]

Truth be known, some theater owners were wary of showing black-interest films. Among them, they used the word *urban* when they meant *black*, and those who owned screens in both intown and suburban locations would segregate their audiences according to the physical location of the theater. (One theater manager showing *The Wiz* at a location where white and black neighborhoods met told me of watching prospective white patrons drive up in their car, see a line of black people standing in the ticket line,

4 Justin Marion and Richard Gil, "Residential Segregation, Discrimination, and African-American Theater Entry during Jim Crow," Journal of Urban Economics, Elsevier, vol. 108(C), September 2018

5 Melvin Van Peebles, *The Making of Sweet Sweetback's Baadasssss Song*, NY: Lancer Books, 1971

and turning their cars around to leave.) Some theaters demanded that distributors of "urban" films provide the cost of hiring security guards. White patrons would complain when black patrons talked back to the screen, and ushers reported being afraid to venture into the auditoriums to demand quiet.[6]

Observant theater owners capitalized in cultural differences. They learned to stock their refreshment stands with extra grape soda when they showed films that appealed to black audiences and told their concession staff to expect patrons to request "extra butter" on their popcorn.[7] In some cities, "urban appeal" films would open on Sunday rather than the customary Friday because Sunday was a heavier movie-going day for black audiences and the distributor could then brag of a huge opening-day gross.

These unsettling observations may not have been universal, but they were real.

It was into this climate that Melvin Van Peebles brought *Watermelon Man* for Columbia Pictures. Columbia, founded in 1924 by the combative and profane Harry Cohn, had fallen into financial shadows following Cohn's death in 1958. A string of box office failures and pressure from the First National Bank of Boston, its creditor, threatened to force the studio into bankruptcy. Indeed, the company's only profits were being made by Screen Gems, their TV licensing division. In late 1968, Screen Gems merged with Columbia Pictures Corporation and was put under the leadership of Abe Schneider and Leo Jaffe. In 1969 they were fortunate to buy *Easy Rider* whose $60 million gross floated a lot of boats, and they were ready to make movies again. Aware of the growing minority market, one of the first pictures they green-lighted was *Watermelon Man* with a budget of one million dollars.[8] The picture was released on May 27, 1970 and eventually returned $1.1 million in rentals (with a probable gross of $2.2 million).[9]

---

6 A discretely worded letter to this effect by the Author was published in Ann Landers' syndicated newspaper column on April 29, 2002

7 Movie theater "butter" isn't really butter. It may contain partially hydrogenated (trans-fat) soybean oil, Flavacol, and, in years past, the toxic diacetyl, among other chemicals.

8 IMDb estimate

9 *Variety*, January 6, 1971

The film's profitability, however marginal, inspired the studio to offer Van Peebles a three-picture deal. He rejected it for reasons he later articulated in his 2003 biographical film *Baadasssss* as not wanting to be Hollywood's "token niggerologist."[10] Instead, he took the fifty-thousand dollar salary and expenses that he'd held onto from *Watermelon Man* and started making the revolutionary *Sweet Sweetback's Baadasssss Song*, a picture praised by Black Panther co-founder Huey Newton as "the first truly revolutionary black film ever made… presented to us by a black man."

Success did not ease Van Peebles' problems with Hollywood. Not only was *Sweetback* slapped with an "X" rating by the Motion Picture Association of America's ratings board[11], it faced *ad hoc* censorship in Boston, not from the city's fathers, but from the theater showing it. Booked into the town's largest venue, the 4,100-seat Music Hall, nine minutes, including footage from its early seduction scene, were cut from the print by order of the theater owner, Ben Sack. In May 1971 Van Peebles sued Sack for violating their exhibition contract. A week later, a Federal judge ruled in Van Peebles' favor and the footage was restored.[12] Whether such footage would have been cut if the actors were white remains speculative.

Much has changed over the last fifty years, and much has not. Van Peebles blew the door open for African-American filmmakers, but the door is still largely closed for African-American theater owners. In 1994, Los Angeles Lakers basketball star Earvin "Magic" Johnson opened a chain of mall cinemas in partnership with Sony-Loews. Designed to bring quality first run exhibition to under-served neighborhoods in Los Angeles, Magic Johnson Theaters was quickly absorbed into the giant AMC chain four years later. As this is being written, the NextAct Cinema in Maryland has been opened by Anthony Fykes and Robert Wright, and

10 Quoted by Tricia Olszewski, "A More Complicated Man ," Washington, DC City Paper, June 11, 2004

11 Van Peebles withdrew his film from the MPAA and gleefully advertised it as "Rated X by an all-white jury."

12 Notes on the film from the AFI Catalogue

the Newark (New Jersey) Moonlight Drive-In has bowed from entrepreneurs Siree and Ayana Morris.[13]

When it comes to newer video distribution systems, black-owned companies such as BET (Black Entertainment Television), OWN: The Oprah Winfrey Network, Bounce TV, and TV One rely on licensing black-headlined shows that ran on other networks.[14] Their models are not yet self-sustaining.

African-American patrons contribute fourteen percent of U.S. cinema revenues, the same percentage as Asian patrons,[15] but are becoming more widely represented on both sides of the camera. At the same time, the huge expense of making movies ($100 million versus $350,000) now makes it even more impractical for films to be aimed solely at black audiences. Melvin Van Peebles' struggles are now being fought by his filmmaking descendants. Although more African-Americans are acting, producing, writing, directing, and crewing than ever before, the system that finances them remains even more obsessed with capturing a wide, racially diverse audience. Will this dilute the message? The real change has happened in television and streaming video where costs are more forgiving and modern white audiences have become more familiar with, and attracted to, African-American culture (e.g., *Dolemite is My Name* was made for Netflix). But while this may be commendable from a human rights point of view, films that address the specific, ongoing yearnings of black culture still face economic obstacles. Just different ones.

---

13 The National Association of Theater Owners did not respond to requests for current figures on African-American theater ownership.

14 Tambay Obenson, Indie wire (www.indiewire.com), Mar 21, 2019

15 MPAA Global Market Statistics, 2016

BLACKING UP, BREAKING IN: "BLACKFACE" PERFORMANCE: RACISM OR STEPPING STONE TO FREEDOM?

by Michael Ferris

EDITOR'S NOTE: Allow me to explain why this essay is included in this volume. Obviously, a major part of Watermelon Man's *significance is Melvin Van Peebles' inverting of the blackface tradition. With the film, he took a form and tradition he believed to be racist (and may be, depending on context and point of view) and turned it upside down. In order to properly understand what and why Van Peebles did this, I felt it was important for you, the reader, to understand the history of blackface. As such, I had planned to write a history of blackface (and other forms of race-swapping as "art"). The essay I had planned to include would have been very different. However, through a chain of purely coincidental events, I happened across this unpublished essay by noted cameraman Michael Ferris. This essay details the long history of blackface. However, the piece goes about this in a manner that I (like you) had not anticipated. It presents historical facts I had not previously been aware of, and in doing so objectively questions whether blackface has gotten a bad rap (in terms of its history). No matter what your opinion of blackface is once you've finished reading this piece, it is a well-written, well-researched essay that unflinchingly poses difficult questions.*

Blackface | 'blakfās |

noun

1 the makeup used by a nonblack performer playing a black role: he appeared in **blackface** | [as modifier]: the blackface components of the minstrel era

Attending a film in an informal setting recently, I found myself surrounded by an assortment of millennials recognizable by their signature tattoos, adolescent clothing and hair color not known in nature. The feature was preceded by a Thirties cartoon depicting a character in "blackface" spouting antebellum Southern dialect. The moment this image hit the screen a chorus of boos poured forth from this agitated and verbally indignant group. They seemed to see in the face of this character posing as a black person something deeply negative. I saw the image as an idiom based on the standards of a past when slavery had been an unchallenged reality for hundreds of years. Since those days, American culture has evolved to understand men and women are not property. America, and the world has come a long way in understanding and forming justice. One basic and clarifying principle must be remembered; behavior must be judged by the era in which it existed. No one in the past survives assessment based on the standards of today. The intensity of the millennials' reaction drew my curiosity. Performance entertainment has always depended on masks, artifice, masquerade and pretense to drive drama, comedy, satire and farce. How, then, has this particular form of camouflage become so objectionable? Masks can be physical, material, psychological, symbolic. So, how do we arrive at the right and wrong of it and by whose authority is it conveyed to the rest of the culture that this mask is unacceptable? Does the use of "blackface" in performance turn one into a racist? Perhaps in the historical narrative there is a challenge to these assumptions?

Reviewing contemporary websites, I found sentiment to be resolutely on the millennials' side. "Blackface" is the "go to" emblem of bigotry today. One website spotlighted "blackface" in absolutist terms, a pure symbol of racism proclaiming, "there is no debate." As absolute as that statement was, it left me thinking about three points:

No event can be judged out of the context of its time.
Standards evolve and cannot be imposed selectively.
Emotions can play a determining role in judgment.

Much of modern culture ignores these principles. That, in turn, invites an exploration of the use of greasepaint in America's past cultural entertainment. The purpose of this essay is to investigate the history of "blackface" in the hope that doing so will provide insight into current attitudes, emotions and thinking.

A starting point is the evolutionary path of the very name(s) used to describe blacks themselves. The current "chosen" phrase, African-American is not the first description of the ethnic minority comprising twelve to fourteen percent of the American populace, nor will it be the last. It is among a long chain of names used during the last century. The word Negro superceded the word "colored." The word Negro carried the authority of science because it divided the human species into three general groups: Caucasoid (whites), Mongoloid (Asians) and Negroid (blacks). As a designation it can be traced back to colonial times and has been in use longer than any other specific word. Martin Luther King, Jr. identified himself and his race as Negro, most notably in his "I Have a Dream" speech of 1963. From the late sixties till today the term has had many revisions: black, Black African, Afro-American finally arriving at African-American. Older blacks prefer Negro and see it as a respectful description. Others see African-American as inaccurate, given that their birthplace is America not Africa. The word Negro is still found in American society today. The US Census Bureau included Negro on the 2020 Census and currently uses "Black, African-American or Negro" to describe this ethnic group. "Black" held sway for a time until the influence of black political groups like the Nation of Islam decided it was offensive in the late sixties. These changes offer vital examples of evolution's influence on history and society.

The saga of "blackface" performance is a multi-faceted, contradictory and ironic story of a bygone era of enormous sweep and consequence that, through the white establishment, brought new freedoms to blacks, a mixture of pioneers, rebels, performers, businessmen, entrepreneurs and victims. They were able to parlay a form of entertainment to their advantage while also living in bondage. It is a history that ranges over one-hundred-and-eighty years of dramatic social change, upheaval and achievement dating from before the jesters of the Middle Ages. The personal style, language, behavior, appearance, clothing, dialect of any class were perfect targets for the kind of humor a rough, underdeveloped, primitive pioneer society responded to. It was raw, unrefined entertainment which appealed directly to a boisterous, rowdy, knockabout population who understood, reacted to and preferred imitation, mockery and satire aimed at those it chose to "cause to seem ridiculous." That humor was, in its time, the dismissive, contemptuous hilarity found in making fun of the world and the people in it. This kind of stage humor had one purpose: to find laughter the common man would respond to and to exploit it. Its enormous popularity provided the evidence of its success.

In America this satirical theatrical tradition was a creative part of New York City, the cultural center of arts and entertainment in the US of the 1800s. The vibrant, inventive locale became the birthplace of an indigenous performance theater that became the precursor to the arts as we know them today. A quaint, rustic form of entertainment was the genesis of the variety pageants, medicine and village road shows, burlesque performances that evolved into vaudeville and then, with the advent of new technologies, into the twentieth century's mass mediums of film and television.

In an "anything goes" society, entertainment was acceptable any way you found it. In the era of minstrelsy blacks were lampooned for aspects that set them apart from the dominant society no more or less than any other ethnic target, be it brown, red, yellow or white. Laughter was the measure of entertainment, which meant these groups were legitimate targets for ridicule; if it got a laugh it made money, and that was the grease that kept the wheels of commerce turning. These standards explain the appeal of mockery which lie in the origins of "blackface" performance.

Whites had imitated blacks since they first had contact with one another. Now, at a point when one man decided to imitate another, his choice and the manner of that imitation ushered in the beginnings of a structured, formalized and completely original form of entertainment that would transform the amusement diversions of much of the civilized world.

Thomas Dartmouth Rice was an Irish actor who performed in New York City and traveled extensively in the pre-Civil War South where he observed firsthand the behavior of its native inhabitants. At one stop, he witnessed a Black stable hand dancing a jig and singing a song in the prevailing Southern Negro dialect. "Wheel about and turn about and do jus' so. Eb'ry time I wheel about I jump Jim Crow." Rice was completely taken by the man's movement, the simplicity of his demeanor and style and especially his joyful self-expression. Thunderstruck, Rice understood instantly that this was the perfect addition to his act; he would mimic the man as closely as possible. He would learn the song, imitate the voice, match the movement, copy the dialect, reproduce the clothing, replicate the appearance right down to the color of his skin (which he did in the show business tradition of the era, using burnt cork to "blacken" his face).

Rice performed his act, which he named "Jump Jim Crow" for the first time, at the Bowery Theater in New York City on November 12, 1832. The act was intended as a "between-the-acts" minor entertainment to keep audiences interested while the bigger stage events were prepared. What Rice and the theater impresarios were unprepared for was the audience reaction and furor which followed. His song and dance was a sensation. The crowd exploded in a delirium of excitement, rushing to join him and participate on stage. Rice became an instant star and "Jump Jim Crow" became an international triumph. In short order, Thomas Dartmouth became "Daddy Rice," the godfather of "blackface" performance and what over time became known as minstrelsy. The word minstrelsy described past times when balladeers, poets and troubadours wandered the countryside providing entertainment as "traveling minstrels" in the Old and New worlds. The birth of the full-blown "Minstrel Show," a traveling musical extravaganza, part musical theater, part circus followed rapidly upon Rice's creation of an archetypal character, the classic "white" version of the slave, popularized and imitated on two continents; America where it originated, and Europe, where it was soon imitated and responded to with enormous enthusiasm.

These events began the "official" life of "blackface" performance. Stereotypes were the meat and potatoes of the minstrel show's characters because they were recognizable to all types of audiences. Early minstrel characters were based on white frontiersmen, mountain men, riverboat sailors and hunters that derived from exaggerated tall tales. Phrases like "whip my weight in wildcats" and "wrassle an alligator" became popular parts of American vernacular. These stock figures were performance gold because they attracted such large numbers of both the common and elite classes. The black slave populace, a visible part of American society, had little chance of escaping the imitation and satire that guaranteed minstrel show creators a sizable and steady stream of ready revenue. Thomas D. Rice had created a performance phenomenon that added another American original to a growing collection of stock characters. Jim Crow stuck as a moniker for the traditional slave (how the name of Jim Crow came to came to represent laws that continued black enslavement is another evolutionary tale.) It was followed by Zip Coon (again, from a song title), an identifiable name for the character of the freed black, portrayed as an "uppity niggra," an upwardly ambitious caricaturization of black aspiration. By now the evolution of the minstrel show was under full steam and there was no stopping this oncoming train.

Once Rice opened the floodgates, imitators began a speedy process of developing this new form of show business entertainment. The Christy Minstrels (a "blackface" group established in the 1840s who were the inspiration for the 1961 group "The New Christy Minstrels") established the basic structure of the minstrel show. It was performed in three acts. In the first, the entire ensemble was introduced, entering the stage dancing and singing a current popular song. The company was led by a Master of Ceremonies who was known as a "codfish aristocrat," a title meant to lend an aura of "sophistication" to a satirical character whose antics prove him anything but complex or worldly. This MC guides the troupe and audience through the show using versions of his attempted humor. Endmen, arrive last, told jokes, sang humorous songs and perform the finale in a cakewalk style of dance known as a "walk around." The second act had a variety show structure with individual performers dancing, playing instruments or doing acrobatics. Parodies of European traditions and characters were common. A black-dialect campaign speech, on any subject, witnessed a character of limited intelligence speaking beyond his ability which invariably delighted audiences. These speakers could be of any ethnicity, but were often blacks who delivered social criticism which had the asset of being inoffensive. The final act, also known as the afterpiece, concluded the production. It became a tradition that this was a skit set on a Southern plantation with song-and-dance numbers featuring characters in slapstick situations.

Whatever entertained the crowds was used by performers who stayed in touch with current affairs, trends, the politics of the day. Take-offs on contemporary events, writers, and viewpoints, including Shakespeare became commonplace as time, attitudes and history expanded the nature of the content. The essential tone was slapstick, leading to crescendoes of ever-rising lunacy and climaxing with pies in the face, rude bodily noises mimicked by inflated bladders and fireworks, all of which emanated from the stage. As is the case with much of history, an irony developed over the slow passage of time. Antislavery dialogue was slipped into these shows along with some defiant messages which were buried so deep in outrageous humor it escaped notice. When *Uncle Tom's Cabin* was published, it quickly became a centerpiece of minstrel shows, touring the North and South as it became enormously influential in the telling of the story of American black people and their distinctive culture.

The characters, acts and the variations that flowed from this moment had enormous influence, serving to bring about small, subtle but significant changes. An important effect was that as black Americans turned out in droves for minstrel shows, white theater owners were forced to relax segregationist rules to accommodate performances. Though capitalistic democracy was responsible for slavery itself, it also worked to bring incremental freedom to large groups of blacks. And, the minstrel show allowed black people to join the ranks of a formerly all white performing culture. Blacks had no reservations performing in blackface and some went on to become famous, well-paid stars. They grew to become creative members of the administrative and ownership class as well. Pat Chappelle, a black impresario and performer, created the Black Vaudeville Show, which was totally black owned, operated and performed. These companies became so successful they were not limited to touring in the east but ventured into hitherto unknown territory in the southeast and southwest to burgeoning crowds of loyal fans.

As the 20th century arrived, the minstrel show lost favor to the emerging world of vaudeville, film and other forms of mass entertainment. The Rabbit's Foot Company was a variety troupe, originally founded in 1900 by an African-American and was still touring as late as 1950. As history would have it, similar to TD Rice in the beginning, it was a white man, in this case a member of another denigrated group, that was present at the virtual end of the "blackface" era. Al Jolson was an actor of great popularity who happened to be Jewish. He starred in *The Jazz Singer*, which re-popularized the long standing tradition of "blackface" performance to a whole new generation. It was significant that this film was also the first "talkie," which made it a draw to that many more millions of people. It is his death in 1950 that marks the finish of the journey of the minstrel train. High schools and local amateur theatrical groups carried the tradition into the 60s, but as civil rights predominated these shows began a slow disappearance from the world of amateur and professional performance.

"Blackface," as a symbol and an influence has had enormous impact, and is still with us. Examples are so embedded in American culture they escape general notice and must be pointed out and explained to be recognized as the precursors they are. Mickey Mouse may be the best of these examples. He is one of the earliest incarnations of this phenomenon. Mickey's visual characteristics, behavior and movements (always singing, always dancing) were clearly modeled on "blackface" performance. He is the complete visual representation of such a performer rendering what had become a classic version of the "imitated black man." Disney's cartoon drawings are a clear imitation; the details of white/black contrast featuring Mickey's big eyes, black skin and white gloves come right off the minstrel stage.

If we follow the historical chain contemplating the careers of actors, singers, dancers like W.C. Handy, Ida Cox, Ma Rainey, Bessie Smith, Ethel Waters, Butterbeans and Susie, Raggedy Ann, Two Black Crows, San 'n' Henry, Amos 'n' Andy, the Marx Brothers, Bugs Bunny, Elmer Fudd, *Hee Haw*, David and Jerry Zucker, we can see the immense influence this kind of performance has had. Modern examples are everywhere: *In Living Color*, Spike Lee's *Bamboozled*, the Wayans Brothers' *White Chicks*, the infamous (and hilarious) Robert Downey Jr. performance (in blackface) in *Tropic Thunder* and the multitude of modifications of hip-hop culture. Add *Saturday Night Live* and you understand blackface effects are everywhere and how permanent as a form of humor they are. The itinerant travel writer Paul Theroux who spent his life encountering the cultures of the world has detailed an evening in Japan at the Nichigeki Music Hall where he witnessed a parlous skit entitled, "Black Cry-Out." He describes a "spirited episode, relating the death of Billie Holiday, with Japanese actors performing in 'blackface.'" This witnesses another compelling example recognizing the fierce potency of an American cultural phenomenon which began small, spread large, to become, through its universal and endless variety, an international influence throughout the world.

The complexities of the history of "blackface" make the subject irresistable. On one hand is the racist aspect of mimicking a culture to exploit their peculiarities for laughs. For some, especially those who insist on the mistaken use of today's standards to judge (and condemn) the past, it is demeaning. But, for historians, who are professionally obligated to ignore emotion, see the factual aspects and observe impartially, it can be seen as a stepping stone to freedom, however difficult its details may have been. This act of imitation turned out to be a substantial first step for black Americans to become part of mainstream white culture in America. Minstrelsy with its "blackface" performers was a means by which American whites could view black people, their personalities, their culture. Author Eric Lott has expressed the dichotomy between opportunity and disparagement as "love and theft," an apt phrase that captures the irony of "comedy" that describes and enables black culture through ridicule. All subjugated groups have had to survive a long, treacherous tramp through history to reach a balance with the dominant culture. History is a complicated progression of gradual advancement that constantly reshapes, redefines the world we live in. With each step, however painful, progress cannot occur.

Does history support a view that through the mechanism of mockery a path was hacked out of the wilderness that helped raise black people out of enslavement? Did exposing their talent, creativity and ambition to the prevailing society push the forces of evolution in the direction of change; where laws slowly altered to make blacks equal to their slave masters? How much does the nature of personal preference, grievance, even animosity and emotional bias have to do with an individual's disposition to see any idea one way or another? Human emotion, an instinctive, demonstrative, primitive and essential aspect of human behavior must be recognized and prioritized for it is. Are these not questions which demand consideration?

Those twenty- and thirty-somethings who saw racism in an old cartoon provoked the crucial spirit of inquiry that insists we remember that understanding demands critical thinking, that knowledge is power and a balanced perspective gives history its meaning. Like curiosity itself, these things are essential and never-ending.

ACKNOWLEDGMENTS

"Interview with Melvin Van Peebles" is an excerpt from *Reflections on Blaxploitation: Actors and Directors Speak*, by David Walker, Andrew J. Rausch, and Chris Watson. Scarecrow Press, 2009. It appears here by permission of Scarecrow Press.

"The Filmmakers Reflect on *Watermelon Man*" contains excerpts from the following sources: "Digital History with Melvin Van Peebles," DGA website; *What It Is, What It Was: The Black Film Explosion of the '70s in Words and Pictures* by Gerald Martinez, Diana Martinez, and Andres Chavez, Hyperion Books, 1998; "Sweetback in the Cosmos" by Matt Bauer, *Pop Matters*, Oct. 15, 2014; "Rediscovering Herman Raucher: The Life, Times, and Return of a 70s Pop Phenomenon," by Preston Fassel, *Cinedump*, November 13, 2016; *Chuck Fries: Godfather of the Television Movie* by Chuck Fries, Monte Cristo Productions, 2010.

"Identity Crisis and Sweetback's Bellyful of a Three-Day Watermelon Man" by Garrett Chaffin-Quiray first appeared in *Senses of Cinema*, March 2003. It appears here by permission of Garrett Chaffin-Quiray and *Senses of Cinema*.

"Estelle Parsons Looks Back on *Watermelon Man*" by Rob St. Mary, and "*How to Eat Watermelon in White Company (and Enjoy It)* Filmmaker Joe Angio" by Rob St. Mary first appeared (audio) on *The Projection Booth* podcast, Feb. 4, 2014. It appears here by permission of Rob St. Mary and Mike White. This is its first appearance in print.

"*Watermelon Man* and *Cotton Comes to Harlem*: Black Filmmaking in Hollywood" by Novotny Lawrence first appeared in *The Lens*, Sept. 23, 2020. It appears here by permission of Novotny Lawrence.

Book design, Robbie Adkins for BearManor Media.

www.ingramcontent.com/pod-product-compliance
Ingram Content Group UK Ltd.
Pitfield, Milton Keynes, MK11 3LW, UK
UKHW062258290726
14090UKWH00017B/768

9 798887 711676